THE NEW EUROPE
(The Slav Standpoint)

AMONG THE MAJOR WORKS OF T. G. MASARYK

Suicide and the Meaning of Civilization
Essays on Concrete Logic
The Social Question: The Philosophical and Sociological
                    Foundations of Marxism
Humanistic Ideals
The Spirit of Russia
The Making of a State

THE NEW EUROPE
(The Slav Standpoint)

Thomas G. Masaryk

New Edition Edited by
W. Preston Warren and William B. Weist

Introduction by Otakar Odlozilik

Lewisburg
BUCKNELL UNIVERSITY PRESS

Associated University Presses, Inc.
Cranbury, New Jersey 08512

Library of Congress Cataloging in Publication Data

Masaryk, Tomáš Garrigue, Pres. Czechoslovak Republic,
    1850–1937.
    The new Europe (the Slav standpoint).

    First published in 1918.
    Bibliography: p.
    1. European War, 1914–1918. 2. European War,
1914–1918—Peace. 3. Reconstruction (1914–1939)
I. Title.
D523.M215 1972   940.3'1   70-124580
ISBN 0-8387-7745-7

Printed in the United States of America

CONTENTS

EDITORS' NOTE

The text used for this new edition of the English version of *The New Europe* was printed by Eyre and Spottiswoode, Ltd., London, in 1918, shortly after its completion by the author in October of that year. A second printing by the same firm, including four pages of prefatory materials and two additional pages of text, was issued shortly thereafter and dated 1918. Both editions were privately circulated to a limited audience. A lengthier text was issued in Czech (223 pp., Prague, 1920), in French (228 pp., Paris, 1918), and German (143 pp., Berlin, 1922).

Details of Masaryk's efforts during World War I to bring to the attention of the English public the problem of Central Europe, the issue of Pangermanism, the future of democracy, and the demise of dynastic rule from the Slav standpoint are provided by R. W. Seton-Watson in his *Masaryk in England* (New York, 1943). Among these efforts was the publication of a weekly journal of the same title, *The New Europe,* in which many of Masaryk's ideas are presented in outline.

Only minor changes in grammatical structure have been made in this edition, so that the document retains the intensity of the author's purpose and its historical integrity. The very conciseness of the original statement, we believe, portrays that purpose best.

INTRODUCTION

by Otakar Odlozilik

The New Europe is an optimistic book. Although
Thomas G. Masaryk began to draft it amidst the chaos
prevailing in Europe (and especially in Russia) during
the winter of 1917-18, he was confident that the Allies
would triumph over the Central Powers. Both the retro-
spective analysis of the causes of the conflict and the
vision of the postwar organization of Europe bear a distinct mark of the author's conviction that people would
draw salutory lessons from the holocaust and join hands
in building an equitable and stable system, to prevent a
resurgence of the aggressive spirit and of greedy militarism.

At the time when Masaryk began to organize his
thought, the situation on the battlefields was not so
favorable as to justify buoyant hope. Political affairs
were complicated by the rapid advance of revolution in
Russia, which Masaryk was able to observe directly,
inasmuch as he moved there from London in the spring
of 1917, some three months after the fall of the czarist
regime. As a matter of fact, *The New Europe,* even in
its revised version of 1918, bears a deep impression of
the atmosphere prevailing in the Russian capital, of anx-
ieties alternating with the deep-rooted belief that the

cause espoused by its author would in the end prevail.

Masaryk's optimism was not unbridled and unconditional, for it did not spring from any ephemeral constellation of the powers of the world but was safely anchored in his philosophy and political convictions. Anyone attempting to uncover the roots of Masaryk's credo would have to move back to the mid-eighteenth century in order to establish his spiritual affinity with the leading representatives of the Enlightenment, both in continental Europe and in the Anglo-Saxon world. Blended with the ideas of Greek philosophers and with the commandments and principles of Jesus were the ideals of humanity formulated by the Enlightenment thinkers. These made the basis from which evolved Masaryk's system. What he professed in the halls of the Charles University was essentially the same set of articles which determined his political orientation, both prior to, and during the war.

Masaryk was sixty-four when he left Prague to work for the liberation of the Czechs and Slovaks. He could look back with pride and satisfaction to several campaigns, in which the right ultimately prevailed over the wrong. Some three decades earlier he supported actively a group of reputable scholars endeavoring to separate modern forgeries from authentic literary works in Czech. In 1899, he attempted, single-handed, to stem a wave of anti-Semitism that swept over the Czech lands after the hurried trial and harsh sentencing of Leopold Hilsner. In 1909, he joined hands with Southern Slavic leaders who attempted to refute accusations of disloyalty leveled at them by a Viennese historian, Dr. Heinrich Friedjung. Masaryk's sharp criticism of documents presented to the court at Zagreb, although ostensibly directed against Dr. Friedjung, had in fact a higher target, the Imperial and

Royal Ministry of Foreign Affairs and its chief, Count
Alois Lexa von Aehrenthal. The conflict in which
Masaryk, then member of the Austrian Parliament, got
involved during the Zagreb trial continued under Aehrenthal's successor, Count Leopold von Berchtold, and
ran throughout the uneasy interval between the end of
the Balkan Wars in 1912 and the Sarajevo tragic event
on June 28, 1914.

In all these campaigns, as well as in many other minor
skirmishes, Masaryk acquired not only political experience, but also confidence that the truth, if solidly established and courageously defended, would ultimately dispel falsehood, and prevail.

The New Europe was one of numerous writings by
which Masaryk defended the Allied cause. It was not
destined to have wide circulation. Although in voluntary
exile, Masaryk was not isolated from people of his own
stock. Thousands of Czechs and Slovaks, who either lived
in the Allied countries at the outbreak of the war or fled
to them when the conflict began, acknowledged him as
their leader. He maintained contact with them despite
many physical obstacles, not least of which were distance
and time, and was able to send messages to his followers
in Bohemia and Moravia. But when writing *The New
Europe,* he thought primarily of those young men who
joined the Allied forces and fought along with them
against the common enemy. Other armies were supplied
with technical manuals—soldiers of the nascent republic
of Czechoslovakia were to obtain from their supreme
commander a searching analysis of the cause for which
they volunteered to fight.

What was the meaning and purpose of the colossal
struggle which was running, at the time of Masaryk's

stay in Russia, through its fourth year? And how should Europe be reconstructed after the ultimate victory of the Allies? These were the basic questions to which Masaryk sought the answer, both to dispel his own uncertainties and to inspire members of the Czechoslovak legions.

Masaryk's wartime writings and speeches show a good deal of consistency in cardinal points. It would not be too difficult to trace the relevant passages from *The New Europe* back to his public statements and confidential memoranda from the early stage of the war. He needed, in 1914, little time to diagnose the international situation and to range himself with the Allies, although technically he was a citizen of Austria and a duly elected member of the *Reichsrat*. He found more satisfactory the constitutional structure of the Allied countries than the thinly veiled absolutism of the Central Powers. He came to believe that, apart from other aspects, the war developed into a fierce contest between the traditional theocracies and the governments deriving power from the consent of their citizens.

His interpretation of the underlying causes of the war became more convincing after the collapse, in March 1917, of the czarist regime and the decision of the United States to join the Allied front. No matter whether monarchies or republics, the leading members of the Allied bloc had some type of representative government and the leading principles of the Enlightenment were embodied in their constitutions. Not bound by secret agreements like the London treaty of 1915, President Woodrow Wilson was free to emphasize the idea of self-determination and to endorse the aspirations of the small peoples, those especially who awaited their emancipation from the Hapsburg, Hohenzollern, and Romanov rule.

Masaryk's first comments on the war and its place in the history of mankind date from the summer and early fall of 1914. He did not share the optimistic outlook of those of his countrymen who expected that the Russians would enter Prague before the first snowfall. Nor did he applaud the oracular statements of Emperor William II predicting an easy and rapid march on Paris and a speedy return of German troops from the conquered territories.

During his life abroad, first in neutral countries, and from the autumn of 1915 in London, Masaryk availed himself of the opportunity not only to study the bulletins from the battlefields but also to observe how the population reacted both to successes and setbacks suffered by the armed forces. A growing conviction that the war would last much longer than even sober analysts expected at its beginning, produced varied effects. The number of killed or wounded was mounting rapidly, especially during the large-scale offensives, and symptoms of weariness could not be dismissed lightly. But Masaryk was no less afraid of a collapse of Allied resistance than of a stalemate and of a lean compromise arising from a desire to terminate the carnage at any cost. In this light should be read the fourth section of *The New Europe,* which has as its leitmotif the crushing defeat of Imperial Germany and of its satellites, Austria-Hungary, Bulgaria, and Turkey. In the winter of 1917-18, the "hawks" in German army headquarters definitely killed the chance of a conference at which the belligerents would sit as equals. There was no alternative to the postwar order envisioned by Ludendorf and his lieutenants than an Allied victory and a peace designed by them.

Knowing that the Western capitals were interested in the preparation of peace terms, Masaryk was anxious to get liberation of the Czechs and Slovaks recognized as one article of the Allied program. He was not interested in halfhearted solutions, such as cultural autonomy within the Hapsburg monarchy, but insisted on a political union of these two closely related peoples and in the creation of an independent republic of Czechoslovakia.

Compared with such objectives as the restitution of the Polish state or the unification of the Southern Slavs, the idea of an independent Czechoslovakia was much bolder and less comprehensible. It was necessary to campaign for it vehemently and to gain support for it both in ruling circles and among the public. Masaryk himself was aware of problems which would have to be solved to make his scheme viable. When objections came, he did not brush them aside impatiently. Section 19 (The Significance of the Czecho-Slovak State for the Liberation of Europe) of *The New Europe* has been devoted entirely to discussion both of the historical background and of the forces that would aid the new nation in its search for security and economic prosperity.

As the subtitle indicated, *The New Europe* was conceived and presented as an expression of the Slavic point of view. When deciding for that definition of his approach to problems under discussion, Masaryk was not captive of vague visions of Slavdom united under one sceptre. He reasoned soberly. He predicted that Russia, if truly regenerated, would play an influential role in world affairs, but he did not wish to bring nascent Czechoslovakia into close dependence on the biggest Slavic brother. He thought that Poland and the Southern Slavic union would be more natural and helpful allies, both for their size and geographical position. While in Russia, he made contacts with some Polish leaders and, after his arrival in the United States, he maintained lively intercourse with Ignacy Paderewski and Roman Dmowski. He had many friends among the Southern Slavs, both among those who represented Serbia and the political exiles from Austria-Hungary. Several passages from *The New Europe* could be quoted to show how greatly Masaryk valued Polish willingness to cooperate in the broader scheme of East European pacification.*

In the winter of 1917-18, the outlook for the Poles was much brighter than before the collapse of the czarist regime. The Western Powers were no longer obliged to talk in vague terms when raising the Polish question. Amputations from Germany of some eastern territories could be supported strongly by both ethnic and historical reasons—since they were, prior to 1772, an integral portion of the Polish-Lithuanian Commonwealth. Neither the Czechoslovak nor the Yugoslav program prejudiced German territorial settlements. But none of the three nations could come into existence without a firm Allied decision that it was not in their interest to preserve in any form the dual monarchy of Austria-Hungary.

Without access to Masaryk's notes and preliminary sketches it is impossible to say whether his call for partition of the Hapsburg domains was as clear and urgent in the winter of 1917-18 as it was in the fall of 1918,

---

*One example is found in Section 20, *The Czecho-Slovak State, United Poland, and Jugoslavia:* "The Pangerman Alliance of Prussia-Austria makes the interests of the Czecho-Slovaks and Poles identical. Without a free Poland there will be no free Bohemia—without a free Bohemia there will be no free Poland."

when he produced the final version of *The New Europe* and had it translated into English and French.

Some facts should be mentioned to help in reviewing the case of Austria-Hungary, to which Masaryk gave much prominence in *The New Europe*. When President Woodrow Wilson decided to join the Allies, America went to war only with Germany (April 1917). The Imperial and Royal Embassy continued to function in Washington until December 1917, when the President declared war on Austria-Hungary as well. That decision affected the President's thought, but when he formulated his Fourteen Points, he did not insist on total dismemberment of the Hapsburg patrimony. The tenth point was not formulated precisely, stating merely "that the peoples of Austria-Hungary, whose place we wish to see safeguarded and assured should be accorded the freest opportunity of autonomous development."

The winter of 1917-18 was a period of suspense and indecision. Attempts to drive a wedge between the Hapsburg monarchy and the Hohenzollern empire continued and influenced Allied policy. While in Russia, Masaryk sensed that far more was going on behind the scene than the press reported. He was afraid that his scheme of Central and East European reorganization might be imperiled by a separate peace concluded after Austria's withdrawal from the alliance. According to a passing reference in *The Making of the State* (p. 273), Masaryk cabled from Kiev to Washington an exhaustive analysis of President Wilson's declaration—an analysis substantially identical with what he wrote in *The New Europe*. But as Masaryk's memorandum could not be located, we have no material for a more detailed examination of Masaryk's views.

In the spring of 1918 the situation changed both in Washington and in the European capitals. The Allies broke underground connections with Austrian negotiators. The journey to the German headquarters at Spa, which Emperor-King Charles was obliged to undertake, convinced the Allied statesmen that Austria-Hungary would not be in a position to hasten the defeat of Germany and to serve in the future as a barrier against German penetration into Eastern and Southeastern Europe. In that atmosphere Masaryk found a more receptive audience and gradually gained recognition by the Allied governments of his political and military leadership.

Pangermanism and its objectives is undoubtedly one of the dominant topics of Masaryk's book. He treated it as one of the underlying causes of the war and as a source of inspiration for those who were responsible for its prolongation. He maintained that the Allied victory would not be complete if only the German military power were crushed. Another task which could not be achieved at once was the suppression, by coordinated efforts, of the aggressive ideology which postulated incorporation into the Reich of other territories both west and east of its prewar boundary. Masaryk was confident that the Allies would be strong enough to protect the western portion of the Continent. Apart from occasional remarks, he paid far less attention to the western than to the eastern neighbors of postwar Germany.

As has been pointed out, he assigned an important role to Russia, which he hoped to see changed by the revolution "both in mind and heart." But there is less on Russia in *The New Europe* than could be expected from the author of *The Spirit of Russia*. Public life there was in flux, and Masaryk apparently reckoned with a long period of consolidation before Russia would be in a position to play an active part in world affairs. Russia's temporary weakness called for organization of smaller countries situated east and southeast of the ethnic German territory.

Masaryk's emphasis on the principle of nationality sprang from his conviction that Europe had reached the stage at which multi-national empires lost their raison d'être. Instead of enhancing security and peaceful co-operation they had become instruments of destructive forces and by precipitating the war had signed their death-warrants. On their ruins, he asserted, would rise governments responsible to legislative assemblies and conducting both home and foreign policy without re-course to militarism or secret diplomacy.

Masaryk's recommendation that the Allied statesmen accept the principle of nationality in redrawing the map of Europe was supported by his emphatic declaration for democracy. He viewed absolutism and militarism as for-midable allies. Collapse of one partner in this monstrous alliance without simultaneous destruction of the other would not guarantee peace and harmonious cooperation of sovereign nations. Passages in *The New Europe* praising democracy were written with emotional fervor. No halfhearted tone could be expected in matters of vital importance. The line between the good and bad had to be drawn sharply.

It would be easy to look for inaccuracies or minor errors in Masaryk's work. He did not write in a com-fortable study full of books and diagrams, but in hotel rooms, or wherever he found a quiet corner. He had no desire to impress his prospective audience with lengthy quotations or with complex statistics. He did not seek

compromise or serene balance, but wrote with uncon-
cealed distrust of the opposite party. The book's mission
was to expose the enemy's designs and to sound an
alarm. The war was in progress and the dominant force
on the side of the Central Powers, the German military
headquarters, showed no willingness to lay down their
arms.

In this new edition *The New Europe* will be read by
a far different audience from those who read it in the
final stages of World War I and at the time of the
peacemaking. What was once a fierce weapon must be
viewed today as a historical document.

The New Europe holds a prominent place among
Masaryk's writings. Some of its invective against Vienna
was shaped by the pamphlets and polemics he produced
from the time of the Zagreb trial (1909) on to the
period of the Balkan wars. His devastating criticism of
Prussian militarism and of Pangermanism had prece-
dents in articles and speeches from the years before
World War I. And *The New Europe* had its continuation. In 1925 Masaryk published an account of his
activities in 1914-18 which he called *The World Revolution*. That volume did not reach the Anglo-Saxon audience under the original title, as its circumspect translator,
Henry Wickham Steed, chose a less militant title, *The
Making of a State*. It is not a mere coincidence that
these two books end in the same profession of faith:
that Jesus not Caesar should guide the nations of the
world in their striving for true democracy and durable
peace.

Since the first edition of *The New Europe*, mankind
has passed through an uneasy period between the two
World Wars, through another holocaust in many re-

spects more brutal than the first conflagration, through twenty-five years of persistent efforts to stabilize international relations under the aegis of the United Nations. The number of the lucky ones who heard Masaryk, when speaking either from the high chair at the Charles University or when addressing a mass meeting, has dwindled markedly. The background against which the ideas of *The New Europe* have to be projected has changed profoundly. Details which had their significance at the time of writing have withered in the changing climate. But the beacon of light, Masaryk's unbounded faith in democracy and humanity, has lost nothing of its brightness and radiant energy.

THE NEW EUROPE
(The Slav Standpoint)

FOREWORD
TO THE FIRST EDITION

This book has a long history. It was originally written more than a year ago in Russia, during the revolutionary disorders; my intention was to make clear to our soldiers the fundamental problems of the war. To our soldiers this book was dedicated.

I turned over the manuscript to a Russian publishing house, but I doubt that the book could have been published in Russia then. In the meantime I had to leave Russia for the West; on the journey through Siberia and across the Pacific I worked over a part of my manuscript into this book, which I now lay before the Anglo-Saxon public. I wrote without being able to consult the vast literature on the subject; only during the last revision of the manuscript could I make use of some American literature. But I repeat that my object was solely to discuss some of the fundamental problems raised by the war.

T.G.M.

Washington, October 1918

I. THE HISTORICAL
SIGNIFICANCE OF
THE WAR

1. THE WAR A WORLD WAR

1. The most striking feature when you ponder upon the war is its worldwide extent. Literally, the entire world has now for four years borne the sufferings of a war caused by an attack upon Serbia by Austria-Hungary, backed by Germany. The entire world has been divided into two camps. Austria and Germany have with them merely Turkey, Bulgaria, and the Papal Curia; all the other states are on the side of the Allies. Only some of the small States have remained neutral, and in them the majority of the people are on the side of the Allies. Thus practically all mankind has taken a stand against Germany and Austria. If the *consensus gentium* was once accepted as an argument for the existence of God, this consensus of mankind surely has as great a moral significance—*vox populorum, vox Dei.*

Statisticians tell us that the total of killed, wounded, prisoners, and missing amounts to 25 millions; those that survive the horrors of the war, the millions of soldiers and their families, and therefore whole nations and all humanity, will reflect on the war and its causes; millions and millions are pondering at this moment, while I write this, upon the war and the situation of nations and of mankind, as I am doing. It is not possible that this gigantic sacrifice of lives, health, and fortune should have been offered in vain; it is not possible that the present organization of states and nations from which the war has sprung should remain unchanged, that the responsible statesmen, politicians, leaders of parties, individuals, the nations, and all humanity should not comprehend the necessity of radical political reorganization. The war and its significance have knitted mankind closer together; humanity is today an organized unit; internationalism is much more intimate than it ever was; it has been created and renewed by this war and at the same time democratic views of society are everywhere strengthened—the fall of Tzarism is but one of the unexpected results of the war.

The unified organization of all the nations of the world, of all humanity, is the beginning of a new era, an era in which nations and all mankind will consciously control their development.

2. THE PANGERMAN PLAN OF WORLD-DOMINATION:
BERLIN-BAGDAD

2. The modern historian, it is claimed, should narrate the history of the future, and the modern statesman should foretell the development of events—foresight being the measure of scientific exactness. During the war I gathered the books of several authors who in the form of stories or political essays foretold the war; but all these so-called prophecies foretold what actually has come to pass very vaguely. In a similar way I, too, fore-

saw the war. Since the Russian Revolution of 1905 I
reviewed my studies of Russia and endeavored to lay
hold of the problem of Russia in its significance for
Europe. To what extent I have succeeded may be seen
from my book on Russia. In connection with this work
I endeavored to grasp the Jugoslav and Balkan problems—it was over these problems that I expected that
the war would come, although I expected it later than
it actually came and not to be so gigantic. In the spring
of 1914, before the Sarajevo assassinations, I took steps
to conciliate the Serbians and Bulgars, because I feared
the hostility of the Bulgars to Serbia in the future war.
My mediation met with a good reception on the part of
Serbia—the fact is an interesting proof that the responsible Serbian statesmen were ready for a reasonable compromise, as, for that matter, was demonstrated during
the tension with Austria in the Balkan war. (I have in
mind my mediation between Minister Pashich and Count
Berchthold.)

My forevision, or rather expectation, of the war, was
based on a careful observation of Austria-Hungary and
Germany, and on a study of the Pangerman movement
and its historical and political literature.

Pangermanism means etymologically the unification of
all Germans, or, in a wider sense, of all the Germanic
races; in a similar way were used the terms Panslavism,
Panscandinavianism, and some others. Today Pangermanism is mainly a philosophy of history, the history of
the German nation and of all mankind; it is an attempt,
through a systematic study of the historical development
and conditions of Germany and other lands, to determine
the place of the German nation among the nations in
their historical development. Under Pangermanism we

also include the political effort and the resultant movement based on Pangerman theory.

The Great French Revolution, with the reaction and restoration following it, likewise the smaller revolutions which were the continuation of the Great Revolution, drew the attention of wide circles to the contrast and the conflict between the old and new régimes, and engendered the theories and experiments toward a better, and, as far as possible, permanent, organization of states, nations, Europe, and humanity; this period witnesses the rise of conscious socialism. Theoretically the period finds its expression in the new scientific historiography. Philosophy of history is cultivated by all nations; history, economics, and all social sciences flourish; sociology is crystallized as a resultant of all these specialized attempts and seeks to become the general science of human society and its development. Simultaneously the study of politics receives scientific treatment.

3. The Germans stood well in the forefront of this theoretical and practical movement; philosophy of history beginning with Herder, and with it history, become directly national departments; German philosophy after Kant is substantially historical (Fichte, Schelling, Hegel, etc.). Socialism, and particularly Marxism, were distinctly historical with a fixed philosophy of history; evolutionism (Darwinism) strengthened this special historicism. The Germans excel also in all specialized social science, economics, and chiefly in the political science of the State and jurisprudence.

Not only social science but even natural science was devoted to the study of the conditions of the German nation. Biology, for instance, speculates as to the proper and cheap sustenance of the individual and the masses;

chemistry serves the same purpose and aims at the improvement of the material basis of the entire national existence. On this broad scientific and philosophical foundation Pangermanism organized itself in recent days as the philosophical and political science of the German nation; Lagarde is its leading philosophical and theological representative; Treitschke is its historian, and Kaiser William is its statesman. A complete system, not only of theoretical but also of practical Pangermanism, has been organized—societies and associations, spreading the doctrine by the publication of treatises, maps, newspapers and reviews, pamphlets, and so on.

I followed this movement carefully; I came into personal contact and correspondence with several prominent Pangermanists, with Constantine Frantz and Lagarde himself; acquaintance with the Pangerman movements and literature led me to expect this war. I wondered that the English and the French paid so little attention to Pangermanism; my own countrymen I warned by articles and lectures against the danger threatening us. I proposed to write a summary of Pangermanism and similar movements and tendencies in other nations, but the war got the start of me. During the war, having been deprived of my library and manuscripts, confiscated by the Austrian police, I could draw attention to this subject only roughly and more from memory.[1]

4. Pangermanism from the very beginning was not a mere theory and political ideal, but also the expression

---

1. I wrote a fuller account of the whole Pangerman movement in the London *New Europe*, No. 1, *seq.;* a general review of the doctrines laid down by the chief leaders of Pangermanism is given in Professor Charles Andler's *Les Origines du Pangermanisme (1800-1888)*, and *Le Pangermanisme Continental sous Guillaume II (1888-1914)*, 2nd ed., 1915. Mr. Adler correctly begins with the history of Pangermanism in the 18th century (Dietrich von Bülow, 1757-1807).

of the political development of the German nation. In the 18th century, the Germans, like other nations of Europe, already possessed strong national feelings; the endeavor to unify the numerous German states and principalities was a legitimate endeavor, just like the desire of the Italians and other nations for unification. The problem became more difficult when the question arose of how to unite the various parts of the nation living in non-German states. Here, it was above all the difficult problem of the relation toward Austria of Germany, led by Prussia; the regularizing of this relation was demanded by a century-long development, especially from the days of the Reformation and the anti-Reformation, when Prussia became the representative of the Protestants, Austria of the Catholics and of the anti-Reformation. Outside of Austria and Hungary, Germans also live in Switzerland; in Russia there have been German colonies in the Baltic provinces from the days of the Knightly Orders and the Hansa; in more recent times, emigration gave rise to German colonies in Russian Poland and Eastern Russia, in the United States, in South America, and in Africa. After the unification of Germany in 1870, Bismarck commenced (in 1884) a colonial policy, reaching into Africa, Asia, and Australasia.

The energetic industrialization of Germany after 1870 brought Germany into connection not only with its own colonies but also with other countries. The United States, Russia, England, India, Austria-Hungary, Italy, Holland, Switzerland, Brazil, and Argentina came into close commercial relations with Germany, the German *penetration pacifique,* as it is now called, has been everywhere very effective. The Germans found plentiful markets for their industry and were able to obtain the necessary raw and partly manufactured materials from foreign lands; Emperor William gave an expression to the actual state of things when he referred the Germans to the seas.

Successful penetration into industries and markets all over the world suggested world domination, and thus strengthened the traditional idea of the German imperialism of the German Roman Empire. After defeating Napoleon III Prussia renewed the medieval empire abrogated by Austria (1806); the Zollverein and Bund were a transition to industrialism and imperialism.

Even during the war I found quite a number of practical men who shrugged their shoulders at Pangermanism, calling it "utopian, academic and doctrinaire politics."

Bismarck regulated, after 1866, the relations with Austria. He managed things so that Austria, after her defeat, was put out of Germany without loss of territory and with only a trifling indemnity; he was thus considerate of the personal ambitions of Francis Joseph and secured Austria for a devoted ally. The Magyars, accepted by the weakened Hapsburgs and won over by the remodeling of Austria into the dualistic Austria-Hungary (1867), became Germany's staunch supporters, and Prussia thus had an empire of 50 millions at her disposal; Lagarde simply called Austria Germany's colony. The Germans of Austria became the most radical Pangermanists, breaking away even from the Rome movement; Bismarck was clever enough to repudiate them officially (*Herbstzeitlose*), but he admonished a delegation of Pangermanist students from Austria to study the Slavic languages if they wanted to dominate the Slav nations.

By the occupation of Bosnia and Herzegovina, Austria-Hungary was irretrievably embroiled in the Balkans, and Emperor William inaugurated an active Turkophile policy, following in the footsteps of Frederick the Great; afterwards Greece, Roumania, Bulgaria, Albania, even Montenegro, were furnished with German dynasties and princesses. The Turkish armies received German instructors, etc. Austria-Hungary became Germany's bridge to the Balkans, Western Asia, and Africa. The Triple Alliance coupled together not merely Austria-Hungary and Germany, but disarmed also the Italian Irredenta. Lagarde and the Pangermanists very forcibly claimed Trieste and the Adriatic for Germany. German capitalists at the same time, in a skillful manner and without much investment of capital, secured the control of many Italian banks; German professors, school teachers, and a great number of less important tourists were effective agitators for Germany in Italy. The older English influences were to a large extent paralyzed.

The actual development of Germany and of her political influence in Europe and in the whole world constituted thus an approach to the ideals of Pangerman imperialism; it tended to establish especially the idea of Central Europe under German leadership—Germany, Austria-Hungary, the Balkans, and Turkey. This Central Europe, having Turkey for one of its elements, naturally extended into Asia and Africa, in which continent important colonies were secured; Pangerman authors therefore spoke of rounding out Central Europe by Central Africa. An Austrian Pangermanist expressed the program in the motto "Berlin-Bagdad," which motto might just as well be replaced by the motto "Berlin-Cairo." The road from Berlin to Bagdad leads through Prague, Vienna, Budapest, Belgrade, Sofia, Constantinople; the same road leads to Cairo, as well as a shorter one via Prague, Vienna, Trieste, Saloniki, then by the sea to the Suez

Canal, and to the English and Italian coasts of Africa.

In the main continental body of Central Europe the Pangermans also include Holland, Belgium (Antwerp), Switzerland, and the Scandinavian countries; these countries the less radical and outspoken Pangerman would unite to the Empire in the looser form of a federation or even in an economic union. More strongly they claim the Slav and other frontier districts in Russia, the Baltic provinces, Lithuania, Russian Poland, and, above all, the Ukraine. One may go from Berlin to Bagdad also via Warsaw, Kiev, Odessa, and Trebizond. The Pangermans recall the ancient Teutonic Varyags and their expeditions against Constantinople, and remember the example of the German Hansa.

The Pangerman slogan frequently points to the Baltic, the Black Sea, the Red Sea, and the Persian Gulf; or the plan is described by the rivers Rhine, Danube, Vistula, Dwina, Dnieper, and by the canals connecting these rivers and enabling German ships to bring goods from the North and the Baltic Seas to the Black and Ægean Seas. During the war discussions were going on about the necessary connections by canals, and many local ambitions and needs were emphasized, such as Munich-Bagdad, Hamburg-Bagdad, and so on.

5. The political push of the Pangerman movement is directed at three points of the compass: West, South, and East; against France and England, against Italy and the Balkans, and against Russia. The thrust against Italy, especially since the formation of the Triple Alliance, was disguised in friendship; the Pangermanists were satisfied to have the alliance with Italy hold secure for them Trieste and the Adriatic. Against France, too,

after the annexation of Alsace-Lorraine, more moderate
claims were made, and the bitterness was mainly owing
to the French *revanche* politics; yet many Pangermanists
threatened to break France for good and all. Others
looked upon France as a *quantité négligeable,* believing
that she now was small (40 millions against 68), and
that she in the near future would be relatively still
smaller and that, like all Romance nations, she had de-
generated and played out her role. In this connection the
Pangermanists were always pointing to Belgium and Holland (East India Colonies); their plans covered the
Belgian coasts of the English Channel, for it is nearer
to Germany than the coast of Northern France, and, in
addition, the Flemish as well as the Dutch are claimed
as Teutonic peoples. There is an extensive Pangermanist
literature about Antwerp and its economic significance
for the Germans.

But in the forefront of the discussions and plans were
England and Russia. The industrial expansion, the building of a great fleet to rule the oceans, colonial politics in
Africa and latterly also in Australia and Asia, and the
avowed plan of Berlin-Bagdad, directed Germany against
England. With Russia up to the time of Bismarck, Prussia had had an advantageous friendship; but when Bismarck attached Austria, and consequently the Balkans,
closely to Germany, and when William developed his
Turkish and Asiatic policies, there was a growing es-
trangement from Russia. The result was that England
came to an understanding with Russia and the fourfold
Entente was born. The Pangermanists are divided; a
part is looking upon Russia as the most dangerous enemy
of the Germans, the others upon England; antagonism
against Russia is found principally among the Baltic

Germans, such as Schliemann, Rohrbach, and others; the adversaries of England are Count Reventlow and his adherents. The Bismarckian policy toward Russia is advanced by Professor Hoetsch and many conservatives; Rohrbach offered a hand to the English against Russia.

The opponents of Russia point to Russia's size and its tremendous population in the near future, drawing the conclusion that Russia is the true enemy of Germany. England, they argue, is separated from Germany by the sea, has no common frontier, is small in Europe, and its other parts are scattered throughout the world without practical centralization; its true strength is in the navy: it cannot therefore threaten Germany, for Germany will have a fleet to oppose that of England. Germany's army, supplemented by the armies of Austria-Hungary, possibly of Italy, the Balkan States, and Turkey, will be able to face Russia and France.

6. The rise and the course of the war were fully directed by the Pangerman policy. Austria-Hungary, as the German vanguard in the Balkans, attacked smaller Serbia and thereby provoked Russia; Germany was "obliged" to back its ally; Turkey and Bulgaria joined the two empires, and Pangerman Central Europe was organized in a military way. The defeat of Russia and Serbia was left to Austria; Germany planned to smash France with extreme rapidity and before England could produce armies; that is the reason why the Germans invaded Belgium. The Germans did not expect the military participation of England, but there they were mistaken, just as they were mistaken about smashing France —they expected to be in Paris in a few weeks. They were also in error as to the military strength of Russia,

were ill-advised as to the Austrian army and its leadership, and never expected that America would join the Allies. But in spite of that the Pangerman plan has been temporarily realized.

Today German Central Europe has this shape: Germany has 68 million people; it has under its control Austria-Hungary (51), Bulgaria (5½), and Turkey (21)—146 million. That figure alone is sufficient to enable Berlin to stand against Russia, which is the greatest state of Europe; Russia, to be sure, has 30 million more people, but its lack of railways, its paucity of population in tremendous territory, finally its backwardness in the economic, financial, and cultural fields, gave German Central Europe a decided balance, not merely against Russia but also against France. Germany occupied Belgium (6½), Northern France (6), Serbia (5), Montenegro (½); in Russia it holds the Baltic Provinces, Poland with Lithuania and the Ukraine, about 60 million. Germany therefore controls 224 million people; where it cannot employ their military strength, it exploits their economic and financial strength. In addition it exploits Finland and to a large extent Russia itself. Russia, being strategically weakened by the revolution, concluded a disgraceful and dishonorable peace—the Schiemanns and Rohrbachs temporarily reached their aim. Reventlow hopes with so much more reason that he, too, will reach his aim. Germany with its central Europe has had from the very beginning of the war the advantage of centralization and unified organization of all its powers; in addition to that, Germany was prepared strategically and politically (the plan and aim of the war), whereas the Allies were unprepared, unable to unite their scattered forces, and had no clear and common plan such as gave the initial strategical advantage to Germany-Austria. Austro-Germany had and has a definite plan, carefully and elaborately prepared in true Pangerman fashion; from William down to the officers and soldiers every combatant aims at the same thing and knows why he is fighting—and such a preparedness of program is a great military force. It is true that the Germans had to change their strategical plans and methods; it is true that with all their foresight there was much they did not know, did not learn, and could not do, but still Pangermanism was of great help to them. Against the Allies, separated from each other, they used with advantage the old plan of Horatius Cocles. After Occidental Russia has been weakened and eliminated, naval England will have her turn—this is plainly indicated by the German push toward the Baltic, the Black Sea, the Adriatic, the Ægean, the Red Sea, and the Persian Gulf.

The Allies have at their disposal England (45), Canada (7), Australia (7), France (40), Algiers (2), Italy (36), a total of 137 millions. As far as military power is concerned, German Central Europe is stronger than the European Allies—the entrance of America since the elimination of Russia thus has a decisive significance, military and economic. The Pangermans are not in doubt about the United States' strength and efficiency; their leading authors very often emphasize the American danger to Europe, and would make naïve Europeans believe that German Central Europe is the necessary counterbalance to the United States and the leader of the United States of Europe.

7. The Germans vindicate the right to their aggressive

Pangerman policy in several ways; in the main it is the right of the stronger which they advocate.

The Germans fear hunger. They point to the rapid growth of their population. Up to the year 1845 France had a larger population than Germany; since that time the Germans grew rapidly, whereas France remained almost stationary. Thus was done away automatically the French danger, but there arose the Russian danger. In 1789 France was the most populous state (France 26 million, Turkey 23, Austria 19, England 17, Prussia 6, Poland 9, Russia 20, and 5 in Asia), and that explains the great influence and strength of France. Germany is now much stronger than France, and the Western nations singly, but she has to face too many enemies; around the year 2000 the population of Europe will be somewhat like this: Austria-Hungary 84 (54 and 30), Italy 58, England 145, France 84, Russia 100 (with Asia 500), United States 1,195, Germany 165. If not all Europe, Germany at least might become Cossack, and therefore the real peril for the next future is Russia; and so Germany must weaken Russia, and, as far as possible, occupy Russian territory for its own increasing population. In the West, Germany needs Antwerp; she needs the district of Briey; in general she needs territory, bread, raw materials, ports. With a brutal naïveté the Pangermans forget that other nations also need bread. "Necessity knows no law," declares Bethmann-Hollweg as the foundation of Pangermanistic jurisprudence.

The strategical argument is of the same quality: the geographical situation of Germany, enclosed by hostile nations on three sides, demands a rectification of the frontiers, and therefore again the annexation of non-

German territory. Ratzel was the one who drew the attention of the Pangermanists to the political and strategic significance of a central location (the fighting impetus from the center, as against fighting power from the periphery, etc.). In general, not merely geography but even geology and other sciences are used in Pangermany to decide questions of right; territory similar from the geographical point of view to German territory belongs to the Germans, and German geographers systematize a special science of geopolitics.

The Germans, so runs the Pangerman argument, are the best soldiers of the world, Prussian militarism is exemplary, the German is a born soldier—militarism and war, moreover, as has been proved by Moltke, are the God-given social order, and therefore the Germans are entitled to hegemony. Darwin's natural law of the survival of the fittest justifies Prussian militarism; Nietzsche gave to the Germans the principal and the only commandment—the will to power, the will to strength, the will to victory.

The Teutons, according to the Pangermans, have the primacy in industrial and technical branches. In addition to military successes, they have success, and in fact primacy, in science, philosophy, music, art, and education. The Germans by virtue of their Kultur have the right, nay even the duty, of ruling the world. The Germans are, in short, the Herrenvolk, the only and absolute Herrenvolk. Germany, so we read literally, will be the saviors of Europe and of mankind.

The Germans by their Pangermanistic plans utilize their historical development. Prussia in 1871, after uniting the Germans, proceeded with the erection of the

German medieval empire, the empire of Charlemagne, the continuation of the Roman empire; Prussia created the political concept of Central Europe. The Prussian-German imperialism and militarism are the culmination of the Roman world idea; Berlin is the fourth Rome, after Rome, Byzantium, Moscow. . . .

The Pangermans, it is plain, believe in materialism, force, and technique; neither Schiller nor Herder nor Kant, but Hegel, Feuerbach, Büchner (Kraft und Stoff), Nietzsche, Schopenhauer, and Hartmann become the spiritual leaders of Prussianized Germany. This materialism harmonized very easily with that national and racial mysticism which the Pangermans derived from the Frenchman Gobineau, from Nieztsche, Schopenhauer, Hartmann, and others; Lagarde even prescribed for the Germans their higher religion, and William believes in his own and his grandfather's Messiahship—the official founder of the Prussian Empire, the plaything of Bismarck, is to William God's Ambassador! . . . The Pangerman materialists receive this sacrilegious teaching with great content, and not even the Marxian materialists of Herr Scheidemann get excited over it.

The Pangermans uphold and spread hostility and hatred against neighboring nations, especially the Slavs; and the Czechs above all, because of their special world situation, are a thorn in the eyes of the Germans. In Pangermanistic literature the Czechs, equally with the Poles, are threatened with extermination and forcible Germanization; people still remember the exhortation of Mommsen that the Germans should break the hard skulls of the Czechs, and Lagarde and the other leaders of Pangermanism speak in an equally brutal manner.

The Pangermanists turn history and sociology into zoology and mechanics—that is in harmony with their tactics of frightfulness, as practiced in this war.

3. PLAN OF THE ALLIES: DEMOCRATIC ORGANIZATION OF EUROPE AND MANKIND; DEMOCRACY VERSUS THEOCRACY

8A. The Allies, not being prepared for the Austro-German attack, were on the defensive both in the military and in the political sphere; it was a long time before they agreed on a common program. At first individual statesmen and governments declared their views and plans; naturally, they emphasized the fact that they had been attacked, condemned Prussian militarism, defended democratic principles, demanded freedom for all nations great or small, and promised the reorganization of Europe.

On October 31, 1916, Emperor William wrote a letter in which, speaking in his well-known manner about assurance in his God, he instructed Bethmann-Hollweg to draft peace conditions; the German Chancellor on December 12, 1916, handed to the American Chargé d'Affaires in Berlin the German proposal stating that the Central Powers were ready to enter into peace negotiations. The proposal contained no definite plan; it was more like the orders of a haughty victor than a genuine peace proposal. Following that, President Wilson appeared on the scene. He had offered, as is well known, his mediation on August 3, 1914, but it was not accepted. After Bethmann-Hollweg made his proposal, Wilson addressed himself (December 20, 1916) to the British Government, as he expressly says, of his own accord, not upon the German initiative. He asked all the warring nations to submit their peace conditions in a more concrete form, since general principles would not do; he himself emphasized the right of the smaller and weaker peoples and the small states.

The Allies replied (December 30, 1916) to the note of the German Chancellor, rejecting it, as it deserved. On January 10, 1917, they replied to President Wilson. In this answer they state that they defend Europe against Prussian militarism in the name of humanity and civilization; they emphasize the right of small nations to self-determination, as was done previously by English and French Ministers and statesmen. The specific political demands are: Belgium, Serbia, and Montenegro must be restored by Germany; the occupied territories of France, Russia, and Roumania must be evacuated and given a just compensation. Territories and provinces that have been taken from the Allies in the past by violence and against the will of the population must be returned; this must be interpreted primarily as the solution of the Alsace-Lorraine problem, but it also applies to the Danes of Schleswig. In the East, Poland must be united and liberated; the nationalities of Austria-Hungary must also be liberated from foreign domination—the Italians, Slavs, Roumanians, and Czecho-Slovaks. Turkish rule in Europe must cease to exist, because it is foreign to Western civilization; nations subjected to the bloody tyranny of the Turks shall be liberated.

The Allies thus insist on the reorganization of Eastern Europe and Europe in general; nationalities must be respected and freedom of economic development fully secured to all nations, great and small. International treaties will guarantee territorial and seacoast boundaries against unjust attacks. The Allies adopt as a matter of principle the formation of a League of Nations.

8B. Soon after the receipt of the Allied Note, President Wilson in the name of the American people (April 5, 1917) declared war against Germany. Since that day, as he has pointed out, and even before that, he has pronounced general conditions of peace.

President Wilson interprets very effectively the leading principles of the American democracy. The principles by which America was nurtured (Inaugural Address, March 5, 1917) are the principles of liberated humanity; the chief basis of peace is the actual equality of nations as well as the principle that governments derive their just powers from the consent of the governed, or, as he states it in his message to Russia (June 9, 1917), no people shall be forced under that sovereignty under which it does not wish to live.

In substance President Wilson thus reiterated the famous Gettysburg Speech of Lincoln (November 10, 1863) : "That these dead shall not have died in vain; that this nation, under God, shall have a new birth of freedom, and that the government of the people, for the people and by the people shall not perish from the earth." Both Lincoln and Wilson repeat the principles of the American Declaration of Independence, July 4th, 1776.

Mr. Wilson formulated the conditions of peace with more detail in an address before the Congress, January 8, 1918, one year after the Note of the Allies; his proposal contains fourteen demands:

I. Peace must be negotiated in the open, without secret international agreements; diplomacy must act in public.

II. Unconditional freedom of navigation upon the seas beyond the territorial limits.

III. Removal, as far as possible, of all economic barriers.

IV. General disarmament.

V. Adjustment and division of colonies; the interests of the inhabitants should be given the same consideration as to the interests of the states claiming the colonies.

VI. Evacuation of Russian territory; Russia is to settle her own political system, and as far as necessary, should receive all possible assistance. "The manner in which sisterly nations treat Russia will be the proof of good will."

VII. Belgium must be evacuated and restored.

VIII. French territory should be evacuated and restored and the wrong done to France in 1871 by Prussia in the case of Alsace-Lorraine should be righted.

IX. Italian frontiers shall be established in accordance with clearly known racial boundaries.

X. The peoples of Austria-Hungary, whose place among the nations we desire to see secured and safeguarded, should be accorded the freest opportunity of autonomous development.

XI. Roumania, Serbia, and Montenegro should be evacuated and occupied territory restored; Serbia should have a free and secure access to the sea. The relations of the Balkan States should be regulated in accordance with political and racial principles given by history; political and economic independence and territorial integrity of the Balkan States should be assured by international treaties.

XII. Turkey should have its territorial integrity guaranteed; but the other nationalities under Turkish rule should receive guarantees of secure life and autonomous development without any interference. The Dardanelles should be permanently opened for ships and commerce of all nations under international guarantees.

XIII. There should be erected a Polish State, containing territories inhabited by indubitably Polish population. Free and secure access to the sea should be given; political and economic independence and territorial integrity should be secured by international agreement.

XIV. A general association of nations must be created securing material and political independence and territorial integrity for great and small states alike.

President Wilson agreed as to general principles with the note of the Allies; in details there were differences, especially with reference to Austria-Hungary, the Balkans, and Turkey. Here President Wilson has been much more conservative than the Allies, but he came near to them in several of his later statements. In his address to Congress, February 11, 1918, he emphasized the principle that territorial changes must be made in the interests of the people, and not of the enemy states; and all well-defined national aspirations should be granted the fullest satisfaction, insofar as they would not introduce new or prolong old elements of struggle and dissension that would endanger the peace of Europe and of mankind.

President Wilson (address to Congress December 4, 1917) admitted that America did not seek to impair and rearrange the Austro-Hungarian Monarchy; but the Government, through Secretary Lansing, declared its interest in the national aspirations of the Czecho-Slovaks and Jugoslavs and, later, supplemented the indefinite text as against Austrian and German interpretations by the more definite declaration that it meant thereby the independence of these nations.[2]

President Wilson is well aware that the integrity of Austria-Hungary is equivalent to German victory. For

---

2. Secretary Lansing's statement, May 29, 1918:

The Secretary of State desires to announce that proceedings of the Congress of Oppressed Races of Austria-Hungary which was held in Rome in April, have been followed with great interest by the Government of the United States, and that the nationalistic aspirations of the Czecho-Slovaks and Jugoslavs for freedom have the earnest sympathy of this Government.

Secretary Lansing's statement, June 28, 1918:

Since the issuance by this Government, on May 29, of the statement regarding the national aspirations for freedom of the Czecho-Slovaks and Jugoslavs, German and Austrian officials and sympathisers have sought to misinterpret and distort its manifest interpretation. In order that there may be no misunderstanding concerning the meaning of the statement, the Secretary of State has to-day further announced the position of the United States Government to be that all branches of the Slav race should be completely freed from German and Austrian rule.

on the one side this integrity would make impossible the President's own program as far as it relates to Italy and Poland, and President Wilson himself has clearly realized that Germany, controlling Austria-Hungary and through it the Balkans and Turkey, would carry out the Pangerman plan, Berlin-Bagdad; and that the whole world thereby would be disturbed and peace made impossible.[3] That Austria-Hungary is a mere vassal of Berlin, President Wilson made clear in the same address in which he spoke of its integrity; and if he ever imagined that Austria would attempt to get rid of its vassalage, he had given up this idea—Austria accepts this vassalage evermore.

President Wilson did not hesitate to change his fourteen peace terms. The government of the United States following France, Italy, and Great Britain, recognized the Czecho-Slovaks as a belligerent nation and their National Council as the *de facto* government invested with the highest authority in the military and political matters of the Czecho-Slovaks; and in his answer to Austria-Hungary he emphasized this change of his fourteen terms and advised Austria-Hungary to negotiate with the Czecho-Slovaks and Jugoslavs. In a letter answering a direct question, President Wilson explained as to his third term, that it does not mean free trade—no doubt, the fourteen peace terms express only general principles allowing more concrete and final definitions and alterations; just as the terms of the Allies at the deciding peace conference will be defined and changed.

9. The Allies and President Wilson did not offer a

3. President Wilson in his address to the Convention of the Federation of Labor at Buffalo, November 12, 1917.

political plan elaborated in all details—the chief point of his proposal consists in a firm declaration for a democratic political program.

Between the policy of the Allies and the Central Powers there is a difference of opinion.

The Allies are democratic and republican states which derive the right of government from the will of the people; they are states that arose out of the revolution; France, the country of the Great Revolution and of the Declaration of the Rights of Man; England, the pattern of the parliamentary régime with royalty subordinated to the rule of the majority; Italy, anti-papal, fighting for the unification of the nation, also accepts Parliamentary principles; old Russia did not fit into this alliance, but she cast down the Tsarism and now strives for a republic, i.e., a social republic; the United States, the first great democracy and republic, which organized political liberty on the basis of ecclesiastical and religious freedom and which served as an example to revolutionary France and to European democracy in general.

The Allies have been joined by other republican and democratic states. The neutral states are to a large extent on the side of the Allies; in Norway and Denmark—even in Sweden and Switzerland—a considerable part of the democracy accepts the principles of the Allies.

As against them, Central Europe is composed of monarchical and militaristic states; this monarchism is in substance medieval, theocratic; Prussia-Germany, with her idea of Prussian Kingship by God's grace renewed the medieval empire; Austria-Hungary, an altogether artificial state, held together by the dynasty and the army, anti-democratic, anti-national, clerical, jesuitical, like Prussia sticks to the idea of the medieval empire. Both states oppose to the will of the people the fiction of divine will, and pretend to be its heralds. Turkey, medieval and, in addition, uncivilized, barbarous; Bulgaria, led by an Austro-German parvenu, who finds every means fair, fits well in the society of the Hohenzollerns and Hapsburgs. The Roman pontifex since long ago led by Jesuitism, works for Austria and Prussia; Austria is the last great Catholic state, and William's Lutheran Germany, in order to hold Austria, sacrifices to Rome and the Catholic Center her Protestant leadership. Jesuitism and Machiavellianism are the politics and diplomacy of papal Rome, Prussia, and Austria alike. The Central Powers became united not merely by the geographical location of their territories, but also by internal spiritual kinship.

Thus we see opposing each other in the world war, on the one side, powers of the medieval theocratic monarchism of undemocratic and unnational absolutism, and on the other side, constitutional, democratic, republican states recognizing the right of all nations, great and small, to political independence. The war, as Emperor William stated, is the struggle between the Prussian idea and the American idea; it is the conflict of light and darkness, of justice and violence, of the Dark Ages and progress, of the past and the future; the Kaiser, with the Pangermans, proclaims that might creates right; the American nation believes with Lincoln that right creates might. America entered the war with the democratic ideal, to fight not for conquest but for the principle.

4. THE GERMAN *DRANG NACH OSTEN*; PRUSSIA AND AUSTRIA; PANGERMANISM AND THE EASTERN QUESTION; PANGERMANISM AND THE WORLD QUESTION

Germany in her beginning (during the times of Charlemagne) was German only up to the rivers Elbe and Saale; the rest of Eastern Germany, originally Slav, only in the course of centuries has been Germanized and colonized by force. Treitschke declares the meaning of German history to be colonization.

The German Empire organized on its frontiers the so-called marches; in the east and southeast there were the marches of Brandenburg and Austria, the latter in the south, the former in the north.

The name Austria means Eastern Empire; the Hapsburgs were for centuries the holders of the German crown and used the Empire for their family aims.

Brandenburg was united with Prussia, and Prussia had been Germanized by the ecclesiastical orders of the knights; later Prussia accepted the Reformation and became the leader of Germany as against Austria.

The medieval Empire in its idea leaned on the Universal Church. The Roman empire has been transferred into theocratic Catholicism, and the Hapsburgs, especially after the union with Spain, became devoted servants of the Church; the land of the Inquisition and the land of the forcible Counter-Reformation made up a realm over which the sun never set.

Austria, by its union in 1526 with non-German Bohemia and Hungary, weakened its position in the Empire; Prussia, being racially more uniform, grew in strength and openly aimed at primacy in Germany against Austria. These differences and antagonisms were intensified by the Reformation—Prussia became the leader of German Protestantism, Austria of German Catholicism; in spite of these differences the two rivals had much in common—both had the same origin from the church and both had the same political aims, to control and

Germanize the East. So Austria and Prussia, the Hohen-zollerns and the Hapsburgs, represent a peculiar division of political labor.

In spite of all antagonism the two rivals finally came to an agreement. Austria, eager to imitate Napoleon and to unify the monarchy by a forcible system of centralization, gave up the leadership of the German Empire in 1806. After Prussia in 1866 by force of arms thrust her rival out of the Bund, which for Austria had been a substitute for the former Empire, she could without any protest from Austria in 1871 renew the Empire. Bismarck managed things so that Francis Joseph accepted with resignation the defeat of Koniggratz, and the latter pushed the frontiers of his monarchy into the Balkans; Bismarck may not have considered the entire Balkan peninsula worth the bones of a single Pomeranian grenadier, but William corrected this policy and Austria became to Prussia the bridge to Asia and Africa by way of the Balkans and the Adriatic.[4]

11. In its historical perspective the German *Drang nach Osten* may be looked upon as an attempt to solve the old Eastern Question. After the Greeks in Europe, Asia, and Africa, after Rome, after Byzantium, after the Franks and the German-Roman Empire, after the

---

4. The German term *Drang nach Osten* is not quite correct geographically; this push is in fact directed toward the Southeast or East and South. In a more detailed study the German push toward the East would have to be compared to similar movements of other nations: The French into Germany, the Italians into the Balkans, the Swedes into Finland and Northern Germany, the Poles into Russia, the Czechs into Galicia, and so on. We undoubtedly have to deal here with a historic phenomenon of a more general nature. This push toward the East would of course also have to be compared with the previous migration of nations from the East to the West at the beginning of the Middle Ages; and finally, the modern migration and occupation of the American continent, Africa and Australia would be the subject of an exhaustive study of the migration and settlement of nations.

Crusades, and after Venice, Prussia, having restored the Empire, continued the task of uniting Europe with Asia and Africa and organizing an Old World, under a single control.

The condition of the world is, of course, other than it was in the ancient and medieval eras; formerly Asia meant to Europe what we call today the Near East. The Far East was in no connection with the Near East, the Near East being racially akin to Europe. The Turkish and Mongolian invasions hindered the development of Asia, but were unable to change the given racial affinities and connection with Europe; India, the hazy dream of Alexander the Great, has been attached to England and partly to France, as Australia became a part of the British Empire. Persia and Asia Minor are reconquering their freedom as the Turkish Empire, step by step, is losing power and vitality; England, France, and Russia have become the real rulers of Asia. Africa, of old in close connection with Asia, also has become a part of France and Great Britain.

The German plan of Berlin-Bagdad is therefore an attempt to displace the three other European nations in Asia.

But the situation in Asia has been changed by the development of Japan and China; to European Asia has been added Mongolian Asia—and both these civilized nations joined the European Asiatic nations.

At the same time in the West there grew up the great American Republic; Canada is now becoming a great country; a new world has arisen on the American continent. Therefore the idea of a Prussian Empire is not in harmony with the present conditions, is obsolete and out of date. The medieval Empire was a great attempt to unite the whole of known mankind into a theocracy; the Pangermans may claim connection with the medieval idea, but their ideas are more narrow, because they are German-national and exclusively economic—economic in a purely materialistic sense. In spite of its magnitude, the idea of a Pangerman world dominion is narrow, small—the Prussian dynastic autocracy and militarism absorbed the medieval idea of spiritual Catholicism. The Pangermans show rather plainly that Germany hopes to become by this war a world empire alongside of the world empires of England, France, and Russia. England and Russia arouse the jealousy of Prussia-Germany; Germany imitates England and Russia, the two principal empires of Asia and Africa—hence the fight with the European-Asiatic empires.

Some Pangermanists are beginning to grasp the difference between the German Central Europe and the world organization as conceived by the Allies and America. They glorify German Central Europe extended to Asia and Africa as the salvation against the threat of Americanization; they cannot understand that Americanization is not merely external, mechanical, but internal, spiritual —the belief in the political principles of the Declaration of Independence, in the principles of liberty and equality, humanitarian principles, in the unified organization of all mankind, not merely a union of parts of the Old World to be exploited by Germany under the guise of Kultur. And President Wilson, explaining the American principles, is not only the ordinary president elected every fourth year—to him, as the expert in political science and history, fell the great historical task of formulating the principles of the policy of the new world, by which not merely the old Eastern question, but all political

problems will be solved. It is no longer the question how
to organize the Old World—it is now the question of
organizing the Old and the New World, all mankind.

5. THE GERMAN *DRANG NACH OSTEN* AND THE ZONE OF SMALL NATIONS

12. From the political and ethnographical point of
view, Europe is organized in a peculiar manner. For a
better understanding of Europe and for a true compre-
hension of this war, it is extremely important to realize
the significance of the peculiar zone of less great and
small nations, occupying the territory between the East
and the West, more particularly between the Germans
and the Russians. From the North, starting with Lap-
land, down to Greece, there is a connected series of
smaller and small nations: the Laplanders, Finns,
Swedes, Norwegians, Poles, Czechs with the Slovaks,
Magyars, Jugoslavs (Serbo-Croats and Slovenes), Roumanians, Albanians, Bulgars, Turks, Greeks. (The number will be still greater, if one counts as separate nations
such peoples as the Ukrainians, etc.)

West of this zone are the greater nations (Germans,
French, Italians, English, Spaniards); the small nations
are few (Dutch, Portuguese), but there are a few frag-
ments and remnants of nations formerly larger—the
Basques, Bretons, Scotch, Welsh, Irish, Icelanders. In
the East (in Russia) there are in addition to the above-
mentioned nations inhabiting Western Russia, numerous
small nations in the Caucasus and at the Eastern frontiers; the center of Russia is peopled by only one nation,
and that the largest one.

The push of the Germans toward the East and South

is aimed at this zone of small nations. Prussia has occupied parts of it, and the Prussians themselves were originally a non-German people of this zone; Austria-Hungary is composed of eight nations of this zone. The majority of the wars of the last few centuries took place in this area, or at least had their origin here; this zone, into which the Germans were pushing from the West and the Russians and Turks from the East, was and still is the area of political danger—danger for the peace of Europe.

The push of the Germans toward the West has been much weaker. The nations situated west of the Germans were protected by their numbers, geographical location, and culture. France, up to about 1845, was more populous than Germany and in general was politically stronger; the Italians, too, withstood the Germans; England was too far from the seats of the Germans, and the way led across other nations; Spain and the present Belgium were connected with Austria only temporarily.

A glance at the ethnographical map of Europe shows this situation: the ethnographical boundaries between the Germans, French, and Italians are straight and sharply cut, whereas in the East the ethnographical boundaries are not straight at all but intermixed, the German push toward the East being marked by the many German colonies actually advanced like forts.

The Western part of Europe is different from the Eastern not merely ethnographically but also politically. In the West are found greater nations and also greater states (the only small nations are Holland, Belgium, Portugal); in the East are smaller states formed of parts of small nations (Roumania, Serbia, Montenegro, Bulgaria, Greece), and Austria-Hungary and Turkey, which were composed of many small nations and states formerly independent. Russia contains a large number of small nations and formerly independent states, but in contrast to Austria-Hungary and Turkey, it contains a great numerical superiority over the so-called ruling nation.

II. THE PRINCIPLE OF NATIONALITY

6. NATIONAL SENTIMENT AND NATIONAL IDEA

13A. The demand of the Allies for a proper consideration for the small nations as well as for the great, resulted from the recognition of the principle of nationality. In order to have a proper understanding of the war and to have a just basis for the conclusion of a lasting peace, it is very important that the principle of nationality should be made clear.

The principle of nationality has made itself felt in Europe with greater intensity since the 18th century, and not merely in the political and social sphere, but also in philosophy, art, and life in general. Since the middle of the 18th century one may perceive in Italy and Germany a growing desire and endeavor for the unification of the nations, divided since the Middle Ages into numerous states. At the same time enslaved nations struggle for unification and liberation; in the Balkans the Serbians, Greeks, Bulgarians, Albanians rise against Turkey; the same thing may be seen in Austria and Russia. Simultaneously with the French Revolution the historians record the national awakening and renaissance of the Czechs and Slovaks, Magyars, Jugoslavs, and in gen-

eral of all nations in Austria, Russia, and so on, and
the same applies to the Germans and Italians. This
process of national individualization is so powerful that
we find attempts to create a separate existence for the
Slovak, Ukrainian, and other dialects and languages that
had not as yet literary cultivation. There arose the Flemish, Norwegian, and similar questions. From the philosophical standpoint the national sentiment and idea makes
its influence felt in all literature; in the 18th century, for
instance, there is the beginning of the study of folk song,
and men like Herder and others strive to grasp in the
folk-songs the nationality, the spirit of the nation, as it is
usually called. At that period also there arose the intensified study of the languages and their comparison: we
witness the foundation of the scientific study of the German, Slav, and Romance languages. At the same time
much attention is paid to history and all social sciences
with the express purpose of grasping philosophically the
substance of one's own and foreign nations in all the
manifestations of spiritual life and of understanding the
development of the nations and of mankind (for instance,
the so-called historical school of jurisprudence, Savigny
—the national economists like List, etc.). All nations cul-
tivate conscious national philosophy; Pangermanism, as
has been shown, is the political organization and philosophical synthesis of this movement in Germany. Alongside of it we find in Russia the Slavophils, in Bohemia
and among the Jugoslavs the humanists, in Poland the
Messianists; in France, Italy, and Scandinavia—everywhere under various forms we see the same movement.
The fact that up to now history of philosophy has paid
little attention to this phase merely proves how onesided,
narrow, and unpolitical school philosophy is, a scholastic

island in the stormy political and social ocean of modern life.

The principle of nationality is new, modern. In the Middle Ages Europe was organized by the church, the empire, and the states; the organization of society was theocratic and is still so to a large extent. In the ancient era the national principle was likewise nonexistent; the various nations were opposed to each other, but simply as stranger against stranger; within the nations themselves, each part stood separate and antagonistic in its relation to the other. Only occasionally the consciousness of nationality came to the surface (as, for instance, with the Greeks in the time of Alexander), but there was no consciousness of a principle of nationality. Hence the political kaleidoscope of the map of Europe throughout the Middle Ages and down to the 18th century.

Reformation and renaissance mark the first stirring up of the consciousness of nationality. The national tongues begin to be used in church services, the translation of the Bible equally hallows the language of the people as against the aristocratic church-language of Latin, Greek, and so on. There arises national non-Latin literature in the fields of philosophy and science, as well as in belles lettres; literature becomes a cultural power. In the political sphere democracy is strengthened, and with it the influence of the people and their language becomes supreme in parliament and in administration; Latin and French lose their political privileges.

Philosophy of the 18th century, like contemporary philosophy, proclaims the humanitarian principle and ideal; the French Revolution proclaims the rights of man; Herder, "the high priest of pure humanity," declares nations to be the natural organs of humanity, rejecting at the same time states as the artificial organs. Europe becomes more and more politically organized in accordance with the principles of nationality.

13B. Nationality manifests itself practically through language, of course the spoken language (mother tongue); statistics of nations are given on the basis of languages; grammarians investigate how far dialects differ from actual languages. There is, for instance, a possible controversy whether German or French, or Russian and German are independent and different languages; but there is also a controversy as to whether the Ukrainian is an independent language and therefore the Ukrainians a separate nation, etc.

The importance of language as the determining factor of nationality is easily understood: the tongue serves as the immediate expression of the feelings and thoughts of men. *Le style c'est l'homme* is true here also. And language has a tremendous social significance—makes possible the contact of man. Nationality, national spirit, manifests itself therefore in literature; that fact is acknowledged generally as to belles lettres—great poets are looked upon as the most expressive representatives of their nations. But even science and philosophy have their national character—even mathematics, an abstract science, differs in the different nations; science and philosophy differ both in content (what interests the different nations) and by method. Plastic arts are equally acknowledged to be an expression of nationality; but the same may also be said of religion, customs, and laws of labor (agriculture and industry), all of which vary according to each nation; there is a variety in cooking, housing, and so forth, in statecraft, and in politics. Thus the Orthodox religion is looked upon as distinctly Slav, Catholic as Latin, Protestant as German; distinctions are made between Roman, German, and Slav laws; differences are pointed out between the Prussian state and the English or Russian. All these problems demand careful examination. We must not accept hasty generalizations; for instance, the Western Slavs are Catholics, and still the Czechs carried out the first reformation—in this brief outline one can merely call attention to the rich content of scientific philosophy of nationality.

The principle of nationality is a distinctive and very powerful feeling; it is the love for the mother tongue and for the group of men speaking the same or very closely related language, and for the soil on which this group lives, and for the manner in which it lives. But this love is not only the feeling arising out of the natural habitual life, but it is also an idea of conscious love; nations have their own cultural and political program growing out of a common history and in its turn directing this history; it is modern patriotism in this wide and complicated sense, different from the old patriotism of loyalty to the dynasty and ruling classes. There is a real principle of nationality, the ideal of nations and not merely national feeling or instinct.

The question of how various nations have arisen and developed, how nations become individualized, is rather controversial. People generally imagine that certain parts of mankind, nations, have special, common, physical and mental qualities; the conception is prevalent that mankind is divided into races (the European, Mongolian, etc.) and races into nations, these again into tribes and still smaller subdivisions. At first, science decided upon a small number of races (five); but as scientific analysis progressed, anthropologists and ethnographers declared the number of races to be much greater.

There is the question, of course, how races arose. To

put it clearly: do they all descend from one Adam? Or
were there more Adams? Modern evolution and Darwinism have not yet given a satisfactory answer.

It is emphasized that nearly all races and nations are
greatly mixed, that there is no nation, no blood strictly
pure; and the question is discussed whether mixed nations are stronger or weaker, of better physical and
mental qualities than those not mixed. What are the limits and degrees of favorable mixture of races and nations? Nations in the course of time change—to what
extent and by what means? Do they change physically by
crossing? By their daily occupation? By living in the
cities? By what they eat? Perhaps even by endemic dis-
eases? And does a change in the body, that is to say of
the skeleton, affect mental qualities? Do mental qualities
of nations change independently of physical qualities, and
in what way? Do these qualities change of themselves or
do they develop under the influence of foreign mental
contacts? By taking over foreign ideas, manners, institutions? The difficult problem arises of how far nations are
original, how far their culture may prove to be independent and self-sufficient.

Such are briefly the problems of the science or philosophy of nationality, a science that has not as yet been
firmly constituted as a separate branch of knowledge;
these problems are studied by historians, anthropologists,
ethnographers, geographers, philosophers of history and
sociology—the great extent and depth of these studies in
the 19th century and the present century constitute a
further proof that nationality is a principle generally
recognized and pervading all life of society.

14. It is very important for the understanding and ap-
preciation of the principle of nationality to determine

more exactly the relation of the nation to the state. The Pangermanists, even though they appeal also to the principle of nationality, put the state above the nation; in the state they see the sum of social organization, the highest and leading power, and frequently they declare that the principle of nationality has become antiquated. Similarly, others declare the church to be the highest organization, others again, the proletarian class. It is my opinion that nation and nationality should be held to be the aim of social effort, while the state should be the means; *de facto,* every self-conscious nation tries to have its own state.

The principle of nationality is comparatively new and unsettled, whereas the state is a very old institution and so universal that many for that very reason look upon it as the most necessary and most valuable achievement of human society.

There are 27 states in Europe (the German states, 26 in number, are not counted here, and Austria-Hungary is counted as one state), but there are more than twice that many nations in Europe. Ethnographers and linguists do not agree upon the number of individual nations. For instance, some join the Letts with the Lithuanians, others separate them; Mazurians are enumerated as a nation distinct from the Poles, and in a similar way the Ukrainians are distinguished from the Russians, and so on. The problems are not sufficiently cleared up and there are no proper statistics; so it may be stated only approximately that in Europe there are about 70 nations and languages (not dialects). This discrepancy between the number of nations and states means that there are many states nationally mixed: states purely national, composed of one nation only, are practically nonexistent. Only a few small and just the smallest states are purely national—Andorra, San Marino, Liechtenstein, Luxemberg, Monaco, Denmark (perhaps Portugal and Holland?).

All larger states are mixed: one can say the larger, the more mixed. Germany (Prussia), Austria-Hungary, Russia (and Turkey) are the most mixed states. The degree of mixture increases from West to East.

This contrast between the boundaries of states and nations, and the fact that the nations in the mixed states are striving for independence, indicate that the states arose by conquest; if Herder calls nations the natural organs of humanity and states only artificial organs, he brings out fairly accurately the function of state against nation.[1] In mixed states one nation is the so-called dominant nation; as a rule it is a larger nation than the subject nations. Only Austria-Hungary and Turkey portray the type of state in which the minority rules over the majority.

The difference between the nation and state has been characterized by some Pangermanists by this comparison: Goethe-Bismarck. A nation is a spiritual and cultural organization—a free organization given by nature; the state, being above all organized force, has been the subjugator of its own nation and of other nations. The present state developed out of the primitive military and religious organization; having been organized by a dynasty and a certain class (aristocracy-plutocracy), it paid no attention to national differences; that is why states are mixed.

The states were formed at a time when the spirit of domineering, of aggression and exploiting, had been ram-

---

1. The racial mixture of almost all nations points to the same fact; here we deal with the nations preserving their different languages.

pant and general; the principle of nationality is comparatively modern and has been established in opposition to
the state. The nation exerts its influence freely (the influence of Shakespeare, Byron, Goethe, etc.); the state
exerts its influence through its power of compulsion (the
influence of Bismarck, not only as long as he was in office
as against the influence of Goethe, but also the influence
of Bismarck's idea after his death). The nation is a
democratic organization—each individual is called, each
one may make himself felt, while the state is an aristocratic organization, compelling, suppressing; democratic
states are only now arising.

Specialists in the science of state find it perplexing to
explain the rise and substance of state. History teaches
that there are two fundamental forms and qualities of
the political organization of society: aristocracy and
democracy. Aristocracy has an oligarchical character, and
a special form of oligarchy is the monarchy, which, in the
low state of scientific and philosophical criticism hitherto
existing, was conceived (not by the masses only!) as
theocracy; the primitive anthropomorphism could not
conceive of democracy, therefore a monarch became the
representative and at the same time the almost deified
wielder of all power (the sovereign). The ideas of God
and sovereign are found together in a strange way. All
monarchies were theocratic, and in the Middle Ages in
particular, the great papal imperial theocracy was constituted. By the Reformation this great theocracy was
broken up into smaller theocracies. Thus arose the modern absolutist states; but in opposition to them and within
them, democracy gained strength. So at the present stage
of political development, monarchical theocracies and the
beginnings of democracy stand opposed to each other

(republics, constitutional monarchies, various attempts of national autonomy, federation, and self-government within the states).

One of the powerful democratic forces is the national movement: the striving of subject nations for political independence and their striving for the recognition of their nationality as a higher and more valuable principle than the state. In Prussia, Austria, Russia, Turkey, the national movements naturally fought against absolutism, and absolutism was the enemy of nationalism.

The difference between the Allies and the Central Powers is the difference between democracy and theocratic monarchies. On the side of the Allies stand republics and constitutional monarchies; Prussia and Germany stand at the head of the medieval theocratic monarchies. Prussia-Germany, Austria, Turkey, and Bulgaria did not become allied simply because they were neighbors but also on account of the internal political kinship. These are undemocratic, absolutist, theocratic states, in which the parliament, even though it nominally makes the laws, has only an advisory and secondary function; political decision and leadership are left to the monarch and his aristocratic co-rulers. This difference, therefore, shows itself also in the treatment of the question of nationality. The Allies declare for the rights of nations and self-determination, the state thus being made subordinate to nationality; the Central Powers are nonnational and even anti-national.[2]

---

2. The word *nation* is also used to designate the body of citizens of a mixed state; for instance, the Swiss nation. The term *Austrian nation* is not used, because there are in Austria too many nations (nine) and its nationalistic struggles are known, although the term might be used with as much justification as it is used in the case of Switzerland, or Belgium. In the scientific German literature the term *political nation*

7. THE RIGHT OF NATIONS TO SELF-DETERMINATION

15. Nationality might have become political power merely as a historical fact, but the Allies recognize the *right* to self-determination of nations. President Wilson declared that no nation shall be forced to have a government which is not its own nor for its own interests. The so-called *Real* politicians, whenever it suits them, are ready to accept things as they are, substituting facts for what is right; but what has been or what exists is not thereby made right—history and social life are the constant struggle of those who defend right and justice against those who adhere to convenient facts.

Although nationality is a strong political power, the right of nationality has been so far formulated but very imperfectly in modern constitutions and laws; in countries nationally mixed some language rights are codified, but so far there does not exist an exact definition of na-

---

is used to designate the whole body of citizens in a mixed state or the ruling nation only. It is of course evident that different nations that have lived together for a long time in one state have to some extent identical views, identical institutions, identical and common traditions; that is why one speaks, for instance, of the Belgian nation, etc. In the case of the Scotch or Irish nations, we must remember that Ireland and Scotland, parts of the present Britain, up to recent times have had political independence, and the people of each used and partly even uses now its own tongue. In another sense again the word nation is applied to Bavaria, Saxony, and the various German states, or to Serbia and Montenegro, and to Canada, Australia, and to the people of the United States; but the federation plan for a closer union of English-speaking nations has proved that the national sentiment is stronger than geography and overcomes separation by distances. I see in the attachment of America to England in this war the manifestation of the feeling of nationality.

Attention must be called to the distinction between *nation* and *people* (natio–populus, nation–peuple, Nation–Volk). The word *nation* is employed generally more in the political sense—the word *people* designates the masses of the nation in a democratic sense. The use of these two terms, especially in the important declarations made during this war, is unsettled and not very exact.

tionality, and the subject of language and national rights has not been adequately determined by any code.

The justification of nationality is found for the first time in the previously quoted formula of Herder. This enthusiastic herald of humanity based the right of nations upon the principle of humanity; the nation, not the state, is the natural organ of mankind. Humanitism, beginning in modern times with Humanism and the Reformation, in both its extensive meaning (mankind) and its intensive meaning (to be human) found general acceptance and became the recognized foundation of all modern morals; the 18th century is the century of humanity and enlightenment; in the name of humanity (philanthropy, sympathy, etc.) reforms are demanded in all spheres of social institutions and activities.

From the humanitarian principle is also derived the justification of and necessity for democracy, socialism, and nationality: leaders and theorists of democracy and socialism, equally with the leaders of the national movement, based the justification and righteousness of democracy, socialism, and nationality on the Christian commandment to love one another. This might be considered rather a tactical argument, but in reality there is no other foundation for morality, and therefore for politics, than respect and love for one another, whether it be called humanity, philanthropy, altruism, sympathy, equality, or solidarity. The humanitarian principle was adopted by the French Revolution in the famous motto: Liberty, Equality, Fraternity; and it was codified as the Rights of Man. The recognition accorded to the value of the human personality is what establishes the civic value and the right to exist of organized social bodies—states, churches, nations, classes, and parties, and their subordinate constituent parts. This is not contradicted by the fact that social bodies are also given utilitarian values— the faculty and power to realize certain useful aims for individuals and the collective bodies.

As soon as one admits the rights of the human person, the individual, one admits also his right to his own language (mother tongue) ; that is a matter of course in uninational states, but in multinational states the official recognition of languages is a matter of national contest and the right to language must be recognized and codified.

With the strengthening of democracy, national tongues receive recognition in the administration of the states, and where in accordance with medieval tradition Latin or the language of the ruling classes of a nation was used, the state gradually comes to employ in its administration languages formerly not used but suppressed. This is true of nationally mixed states, such as Austria and Russia.[3]

The mother tongue, as a means of intercourse, is intimately associated with the thoughts, feelings, and the entire spiritual and cultural life of individuals and nations. To the extent to which all nations in Europe participated in promoting culture, the various languages became richer and more valuable from the cultural point of view, and the result is the growing, cultural equality of languages in analogy to political and international equality in the rights of nations. Modern means of communication made possible the achievement of a cultural unity among the

---

3. That explains why democratic movements, especially revolutions, promoted the language of the masses; during the French Revolution, for instance, important state acts were published in Provençal; and it is known how deeply the French Revolution affected style and rhetoric. The literary use of various dialects also can be explained by popular political movements, etc. The Russian revolution is very interesting in its influence on the various smaller nations in Russia.

dismembered parts of nations ruled by various states; nationality became a conscious force, language its practical exponent, and social literature in its widest meaning became the expression and the most valuable organ of nationality.

That is why the political dependence of nations and parts of nations in mixed states is so keenly felt and so strongly and so generally resented. What extremely barbarian act it was to cut the Polish nation into three parts and to forbid even children to speak Polish, as was done in Prussia and Russia! By what right are the Poles, Czechs, and Slovaks oppressed politically, when other and smaller nations (Danes, Dutch, and other) are free? And it is not quite absurd to have the Roumanian in Roumania free, while his neighbor and brother in Hungary is oppressed? Why should the Albanians have their own state, and the Jugoslavs not?

This disparity in the official valuation of nationality and state is based on the medieval valuation of states, consecrated by the church; this valuation was taken over by modern absolutism. This absolutism was sustained by dynasties and aristocracies; but when in the 18th century the Great Revolution (a revolution that was not political only, but also moral and intellectual) organized democracy and republicanism, when absolutism, monarchism, and aristocratism were weakened, then nationality and the language of the people also came to be recognized in the administration of the state. The theocratic overvaluation of the state—and that meant practically of the sovereign —apotheosis of these gave way to a democratic valuation; the state becomes the central organ of administration, not of aristocratic domination, and therefore becomes also the instrument of the nations and of their cultural endeavors. Today all European nations struggle for liberation and political unity, for the political organization of Europe on the basis of nationality. The intrinsic historical connection of democracy with nationality explains why the democratic states, France, England, Italy, and so on, and now revolutionary Russia, declare solemnly in favor of the right of all nations to self-determination.

And it is equally clear why militaristic monarchies of the medieval type, why Prussia-Germany, Austria, and Turkey (Ferdinand of Bulgaria fits in well with this trinity) oppose the principle of nationality, placing the state above the nation and arguing from their narrow etatism that the Allies have no business to interfere in the "internal" affairs of their states.

The self-determination of nations cannot, of course, be realized as long as this pharisaic principle is respected. A great German newspaper declared the slaughter of the Armenians to be an "internal" affair of Turkey. The oppression of Slavs, Roumanians, and Italians in Austro-Hungary is also claimed to be an internal affair, and so is the cultural murder of the Poles in Prussia. And yet these "internal affairs" gave rise to the present "outward" world war.

By the Allies' note to President Wilson questions of nationality became international questions. The question of Belgium, Serbia, and the Jugoslavs in general; of Alsace-Lorraine; of the Danes and of Schleswig; of the Italians, Roumanians, Czecho-Slovaks, and Slavs in general in Austria-Hungary, and that of the Poles are international problems, problems of Europe and humanity. Pangermanists, of course, deride now all humanitarian ideals, even though they have been proclaimed by the greatest and best Germans; one of their prominent leaders, Professor Haase, declares expressly that love for one's neighbor can exist only as between individuals, but cannot be at all thought of as between nations. On this moral foundation the Pangermanists formulate their aggressive, purely militaristic demands: the Germans must arrange their frontiers; the Germans must provide bread for their growing population; the Germans are surrounded by foreign nations, and therefore they must be militarists, and so on. As if other nations likewise did not have unfavorable frontiers or were not surrounded by foreigners (as, for instance, we, the Czechs), or do not have to provide for food. No, it is either Kant or Bismarck, either Schiller or William, either Lessing or Bernhardi! Czar William constantly appeals to God and declares himself to be God's instrument, to Jesus, of course, he does not appeal; this Prussian Jahveh is in reality the political power of a state-recognized and privileged church which gives to the Czar and his state a pastor for each village as God's gendarme. It has been stated above that European states are still theocratic, therefore democracy everywhere is opposed to the state and the church. Democracy has a human foundation, and not a divine foundation in the theocratic sense; it has its foundation in morality, not in official religion. Only insofar as morality—love for one another—is hallowed by true, pure, nonpolitical religion, does democracy recognize politics subspecie aeternitatis. Such politics is possible on the basis of the teachings of Jesus and of his two great commandments, and only on that basis.[4]

---

4. The fundamental idea of the historical antithesis between democracy and theocracy already exposed is set forth at length in my book on Russia.

8. THE PROBLEM OF SMALL NATIONS AND STATES; THE FEDERATION OF SMALL NATIONS

16. The definition and significance of Great Powers has changed much in recent years; fewer Great Powers are now recognized; old ones step aside and new ones take their places. The standard of greatness has become relative by the growth of the population. The Pangermanists recognize only three, at most four, Great Powers in Europe—Germany, Russia, Great Britain, and perhaps France; many will not even recognize France as a Great Power. Those who emphasize the previously mentioned natural weaknesses of Russia (the contrast of the inadequate number of the population with the vast uncultured territory, and the like) speak only of two Great Powers, Germany and Great Britain; from this point of view Germany frequently is declared to be the Great Power par excellence, and therefore the natural and predestined master of Europe and the world.

The Pangermanists appeal to history, claiming that evolution leads to the organization of great nonnational, mixed states; there have even been writers who declare mixed states to be a higher type than purely national states. The German Social Democrats here agree with the Pangermanists on the ground that greater territories are needed to accomplish the economic and social reforms of Marxian Socialism. In general, the public political opinion of Europe favors great states. The watchword is imperialism. Smaller states and nations are spoken of with pity or a sort of contempt. The German view of a state as a power was formulated by Treitschke, when he said that there is something ridiculous in the idea of a small state.

Let us see what history tells us. Now and then, great nationally mixed states have been organized. The last attempt was made by Napoleon; before him was the medieval Empire, the Franks, Rome, Byzantium, and so on, as we go backward. All these empires perished, and out of them arose smaller states. The medieval Empire was a peculiar alliance of various states and the church, and in general, the composition of these great empires varied greatly. On the whole, great multinational empires are an institution of the past, of a time when material force was being cherished and the principle of nationality had not been recognized, because democracy had not been recognized. Great multinational empires and autocracy are almost synonymous.

History teaches that some new great states arose by the union of smaller states of the same nationality— Germany, Italy. The growth of these states is something very different from the subjugation of various nations by one nation.

History also teaches that in modern times alongside the few greater states arising through national unification, there arose many more small states; since the end of the 18th century we have witnessed the birth of Belgium, Serbia, Greece, Bulgaria, Norway, Albania (Switzerland was reorganized). Nonnational Great Powers are decaying; Turkey has fallen; just now the greatly mixed Russia is already dismembered, giving rise to smaller and small states; and nonnational Austria-Hungary is following her example.

History teaches that evolution very decidedly favors the rise of smaller national states. Out of 27 states in Europe, only Russia, Germany, Austria-Hungary, England, France, and Italy may be accepted as large states; the others, therefore a great majority, are smaller, either of moderate size like Spain or small like Denmark and Montenegro. The assertion of the Pangermanists and Marxists is quite patently not justified.

Quite erroneous is the identification of imperialism with capitalism as the Marxists make it: the great empires arose before modern capitalism, and imperialistic and aggressive designs cannot be traced merely to financial and economic motives.[5]

17. The modern state, having far more complicated aims than the older state, needs a great deal of money, to express it briefly; the citizen is obliged, in addition to his home and private needs, to give up a considerable part of his income and earnings to the administration of the state. All countries are not equally rich and fertile, do not possess equally favorable geographical locations or equally good neighbors—so it is natural that the smaller, less rich states and nations (whether by nature or by their degree of economic and cultural development) cannot afford to their citizens all the advantages which may be found in the richer and larger states. But where is it written that all nations must be equally rich or that they must be equal in general?

A small nation may intensify all its work and thereby

---

5. As far as the conception of imperialism is concerned, I desire to call attention at least to the following: Imperium can be conceived in the Roman sense or in the medieval sense: the Roman Empire is the creation of expansive militarism; the medieval imperium was in theory, and at first in fact also, built on a spiritual foundation—the Empire was theocratic, the state and church were one. Later the political empire (the Emperor) grew stronger than the papacy, and in modern times, the various states actually took for their own all medieval absolutism; the dynasties still hold on to the theocratic foundation. Austria, after making intensive use of the medieval Empire for its dynasty, gave the Empire up; Prussia renewed it; Russia held on to the idea of the Byzantine Empire. In practice, all these Empires followed the old Roman example —material domination was to them both the means and the end. The medieval Empire had some justification during a certain time; the modern empire is an anachronism.

Often the term imperialism is used, when some kind of peaceful federation of various states is thought of. Cf. the chapter on state nationalism.

make up to a large extent its lack of numbers; a large nation proceeds in all its activities rather extensively. One may compare it to the economic exertions as between the owner of a small piece of land and one who is the owner of a great estate. Therefore in the large states individual parts claim various forms of autonomy against centralization.

The adversaries of small nations and states emphasize that small states do not prosper, not merely from the economic and military point of view, but also in the matter of culture—the small nation is said to have small and stunted ideas and ideals. This claim must be settled by carefully ascertaining the facts and clearing up the concepts. Let us, for example, take the Czechs; a nation far smaller than the Germans (the figures now are about 10 to 80) managed to hold its own against the strong German pressure for centuries and continues to do so down to this day, although the Slavs who settled farther west and north have been Germanized. Politically Bohemia occupied an important place in the family of nations and played for a time even imperialistic politics, having incorporated German-Austria with Vienna and even Brandenburg, where Berlin lies to-day. In culture Bohemia was eminent as early as the 14th century; and the Czechs were the first to break the authority of the medieval theocracy and to open the new era by their reformation; the names of Zizka, Hus, Chelcicky, and Comenius are among the greatest. When they had been beaten by the united effort of all Europe, the Czechs, after merely existing for 200 years, roused themselves at the end of the 18th century to new cultural life—the renaissance of the Czecho-Slovak nation is proof of strong national vitality. Why, therefore, and by what right do the Pangermanists deny the Czechs and Slovaks independence? The present-day great nations have laid the foundation of their culture at a time when they were smaller or as small; and it is especially significant that in the former days there did exist the modern methods of communication, industry, and the like, which are said to be necessary for the development of the up-to-date culture, but these conditions now are just as accessible to the small nations as to the great. Dante, Shakespeare, Molière, and others lived in the days of small things. And Jesus and His followers grew up in a small remote Asian region. Just like the Czech nation, so grew the Danes, Norwegians, Swedes, Finns, and their like, constituting the proof that cultural accomplishments cannot be measured merely by square miles of territory or statistical figures.

A more exact analysis and comparison of great and small nations would have to take into account the natural endowment and capacity of the various nations; in that respect the intensive effort of many small nations is evidence of a considerable natural endowment. A small nation, defending itself against a large nation, thinks far more intensively than its great neighbor, who relies more on his numerical superiority. The current opinion of the cultural degree and accomplishment of nations is very inexact and unscientific. (According to measurements of even German anthropologists, the Czechs, and I believe the Croatians, show the highest skull and brain index.)

18. The opponents of small states and nations point to Austria as the classic demonstration that small nations must unite themselves into larger federated bodies, and as a proof that they cannot maintain their independence. It is true that the Turkish danger brought about in

1526 the union of Austria, Bohemia, and Hungary; but it is equally true that the Austrian Hapsburgs very shortly abused the free union and oppressed both Bohemia and Hungary. The Hapsburgs became the right arm of the threatened theocracy and broke, with the help of Empire and Europe, Bohemia and her Hussite Revolution. With blood and iron and Jesuitism the Hapsburgs crushed the Czech Revolution (1618) and culture. The whole history of Austria and her efforts for a uniting, centralizing and Germanizing state is proof and example of dynastic domination, but of no federation of nations. Austria was a federation only as long as it was the union of three free states; Austria-Hungary of today is not a federation of small nations. Such a federation can be found only in the writings of weak-minded courtier-historians and politicians: Austria-Hungary is the organized oppression of the majority by the minority; Austria-Hungary is the continuation of medieval dynastic absolutism.

The Dual Monarchy is composed of nine nations: Germans, Czechs with the Slovaks, Poles, Ukrainians, Serbo-Croats, Slovenes, Roumanians, Italians, Magyars. Some count the Slovaks as a separate nation; the Latins in the Tyrol are a separate nation, and a part of the Jews claim again nationality. In all other nationally mixed states, even in Russia, the so-called ruling nation is in the majority; only in Austria and Hungary does the minority rule over the majority. What is Austria? A dynasty with the aristocracy, the army and its higher officers, the higher bureaucracy and the church (hierarchy) furnishing the necessary spiritual police. Mickiewicz properly compares this anti-national state to the East India Company, in which 200 families exploit the nations.

Turkey also was a "federation" of nations—and she fell; with Turkey will also fall the anomaly of Austria, as Mazzini correctly foretold.

A real federation of nations will be accomplished only when the nations are free to unite of their own accord. The development of Europe points to that end. The program of the Allies answers fully to this development: free and liberated nations will organize themselves, as they find necessary, into greater units, and thus the whole continent will be organized. Should there be federations of smaller states, they will be federations freely entered upon, out of the real needs of the nations, not out of dynastic and imperialistic motives. Federation without freedom is impossible; that must be emphatically stated to those Austrian and other politicians who are promising autonomy and federation. We have now three examples of federated states, and in all three instances they are free indipendent states that have become federated: Switzerland, America, and even Germany. Switzerland and America are republics; Germany is a monarchy, but her single states are independent. Do the Hapsburgs want a real federation of independent states and nations? Surely not; in any case the Germans threatened that they would not permit a federalization of Austria.

According to the program of the Allies, the small nations and states shall be treated with the same respect politically and socially as the great nations and states. A small nation, an enlightened and culturally progressing nation, is just as much a full-fledged unit and cultural individual as a great nation. The problem of small nations and states is the same as the problem of the so-called small man; what matters is that the value of the man, the individuality of the man, is recognized without regard to his material means. This is the proper sense and kernel of the great humanitarian movement which characterizes modern times, as manifested in socialism, democracy, and nationalism. The modern humanitism recognizes the right of the weak—that is the meaning of all efforts for progress and for the recognition of human dignity: the strong will always help himself. The protection of the weaker and the weak, the protection of the small, of the individual, of corporations and classes, of nations and states—that is the task of modern times. Everywhere the weak, oppressed, and exploited unite themselves—association is the watchword of our era: federation, the free federation of small nations and states will be the consummation of this principle securing the final organization of the whole of mankind.[6]

9. NATIONALITY AND INTERNATIONALITY

19. Enemies of small nations point to the tendency of the historical development which, according to them, aims at the formation of large states in which the small, national states are merged; at the same time they lay stress on the value of internationalism and condemn small nations and states as tedious obstacles to international universalism.

The supposed tendency of progress favoring the for-

6. The problem of federation (and self-government) demands a more detailed explanation than can be given in this sketch. It is hardly necessary to call attention to the difference between the American and German federations, which are substantially uni-lingual, and the federation of three (4) nations; but it is important to state that the advocates of federations do not anticipate the great changes which will be brought about after the war. If Europe will accept the democratic ideas of the Allies, federation will be easier, or rather less necessary, because the whole of Europe will be more closely organized.

mation of great states has already been discussed; it remains to examine the assertion about internationalism and its relation to nationality.

That the smaller and small nations should become independent is not contrary to the tendency of the development which makes interstate and international relations ever closer and closer; individuals and nations, it is true, have a direct need for union with others, and history aims at the organization of all mankind.

This historical development is a double process: together with the individualization of all departments the organization of individuals is taking place. Politically expressed, there is going on the development of autonomy and self-government of individuals, classes, nations; and at the same time individuals, classes, and nations are uniting closer, are being organized and centralized. This process goes on within the nations themselves, but also between one nation and another—interstatism and internationalism become more intimate. Europe emphatically tends toward a continental organization.

The principle of nationality stands alongside the international (interstate) principle. The European nations, while becoming individualized, tend to draw closer together economically and with respect to communication (railroads, and so forth) and their entire technical culture; but individualization and centralization are deepened also spiritually by a growing interchange of ideas and of all culture (knowledge of foreign languages, translation, and the like). Europe and humanity are becoming more unified.

Between nationality and internationality there is no antagonism, but on the contrary, agreement: nations are the natural organs of humanity. Humanity is not supernational, it is the organization of individual nations. If, therefore, individual nations struggle for their independence and attempt to break up states of which they have heretofore been parts, that is not a fight against internationality and humanity, but a fight against aggressors, who misuse states for the purposes of leveling them and enforcing political uniformity. Humanity does not tend to uniformity, but to unity; it will be the liberation of nations which will make possible the organic association, the federation of nations, of Europe, and of all mankind.

The diversity of languages is not an obstacle. In the Middle Ages, and even during a long part of the Modern Era, Latin was the international tongue; in modern days it was displaced by French, to the extent that France politically and culturally held the leadership of Europe. Today the English language is the most widely spread, not merely in Europe, but also in the other continents; the growth of the English nation accounts for it.

Today the knowledge of languages is widely spread in all nations, and especially among the small nations; men able to speak two languages are more numerous every day, and that renders intimate intercourse among nations possible. During the prevalence of French or Latin this intercourse was not more perfect, but quite the contrary; the knowledge of these tongues was limited to the educated classes and the nobility. Today education and also the knowledge of languages is more general, more democratic.

Internationalism of today is something different from the cosmopolitanism of the 18th century; it was an aristocratic cosmopolitanism limited to the nobility and the educated classes. In the 20th century, in addition to the French and English, other nations and their languages achieved prominence (German, Italian, Russian), and at the same time the improved means of communication and the evergrowing intermigration of nations, especially of working men, strengthened democratic international- ism. The socialist "International" is its peculiar organ; but today not merely the working men, but all classes— scientists and philosophers, engineers, merchants, lawyers, artists—are organized internationally.

This internationalism makes possible a division and organization of labor of the nations, not merely economic labor, but all cultural labor. Europe and humanity are becoming more unified. Internationalism is not impeded by small nations, as was proved even in this war.

10. POLITICAL INDEPENDENCE AND NATIONAL AUTONOMY

20. Political independence is for an enlightened, civ- ilized nation a vital need—politically dependent nations have even in the most civilized states been oppressed and exploited economically and socially. The more thought- ful and energetic the nation, the more it feels its sub- jection; and there are cases where the political master is less educated, less efficient, than the subject people. The greatest Polish poets gave a very penetrating analy- sis of the constant revolutionary sentiment of an oppressed enlightened nation; Mickewicz summed it up in the words "The only weapon of a serf is treason." The forcible suppression and denationalization is a tre- mendous loss of energy, a lowering of the moral level; it hurts also the dominant oppressing nation in that it commits violence and does not amalgamate with itself the best characteristics of the oppressed nation. The

Hungarian State, with its Magyarization by violence, is an ugly example of the deterioration of character by forcible denationalization.

Political independence is, of course, becoming more and more relative, but that is no argument against the concession of independence to oppressed nations. The former sovereignty of absolute states is passing away by the growing interstatism and internationalism; that sovereignty was, to a large extent, conditioned by isolation. Contemporary political alliances are a manifest weakening of former sovereignty. It may be admitted that small states feel the pressure of large neighbors—an example may be seen in the relations of Austria-Hungary to the Balkan States. It has been, therefore, often suggested that it would be better for small states and nations if they became directly a part of the large hostile states; Serbia —so its adversaries said—would, if annexed by Austria-Hungary, increase the number of the Jugoslavs and even unify them, and would oppose its enemy more efficiently than as an independent state.

These and similar counsels are derived from the principles of contemporary Machiavellian politics. The development of Europe and humanity tends toward democratization, that is, humanization of interstate and international relations; politics will cease to be carried on on Machiavellian principles; national independence and self-existence will freely develop along with increasing internationalism.

In recent days champions of the existing great mixed states, principally of Austria-Hungary, proposed national autonomy as the means for solving national questions; that is also the program of many socialists. (The Austrian socialists Springer, Renner, and Bauer give a detailed program, but in England and in other countries also some socialists, even during the war, recommended similarly national autonomy.)[7]

National autonomy honestly carried out, recognition of language rights in schools, public offices and parliament, may be sufficient in certain cases, especially for national minorities, but it is not sufficient for national majorities and nations, such as the Czecho-Slovaks, Poles, and others, who by sheer violence were deprived of their independence and are striving to regain it.

11. RADICAL RECONSTRUCTION OF EUROPE ON THE FOUNDATION OF NATIONALITY; NATIONAL MINORITIES

21. Europe has been organized by states and churches and has been organized in days when the principle of nationality was not accorded the recognition that it obtains in modern times, and for that reason, as was already pointed out, nearly all the states are nationally mixed, and are now disturbed by the problem of nationality.

Many statesmen of a conservative turn of mind, while admitting the justice of the principle of nationality, advocate a nonradical solution of national problems; and they agree to the formation of certain new national states, but favor the maintenance, as far as possible, of the political *status quo* by proposing to solve the national problems to the largest possible extent by national and language autonomy.

---

7. A distinction is made between territorial autonomy for territories inhabited by one nation, and personal autonomy for scattered small minorities after the manner of the present religious minorities. In Bohemia both the Czechs and the Germans in various proposals recognized minorities, when they amount to 20 and 25 percent.

Much has already been said of autonomy. It is true that some nations, smaller and less highly developed, would be satisfied with autonomy, at least for the time being; it is true that there are several nations that have no national and political aspirations at all. So, for instance, the Flemish declared during this war that they do not want to be separated from their Walloon fellow-citizens. But it is not a question of nations like these, but rather of nations who will not be satisfied with autonomy in a foreign state and who demand political independence.

If Europe is to be truly democratic, and if we are to have a permanent peace, a more radical solution of national problems is necessary. Nevertheless, as things are, it is to be expected that even in the reconstructed Europe there will be national minorities, and therefore mixed states. The problem is to make these minorities as small as possible. But when two nations (Belgium) or three (Switzerland), themselves decide to maintain their mixed state, the will of such national parts will surely be respected.

National difficulties and struggles are to a large extent questions of national minorities. For instance, the Poles in Prussia form a minority of all Prussia; but in the Polish territory of Prussia there are again German minorities, and similar conditions exist elsewhere. Very important is the problem of minorities scattered here and there on territory of another nation, as in cities or industrial centers. Such minorities will remain even in the reconstructed states. The rule for reconstruction must be to have the minorities as small as practicable, and to have them protected in their civic rights. It would therefore be desirable that the Peace Congress should adopt an international agreement for the protection of national minorities; perhaps there could be erected an international arbitration tribunal for national questions.

The Pangermans often proposed the transmigration of quite large national minorities; the example of the Zionists and emigration in general suggest these means. It is doubtful whether it may be carried out without compulsion and injustice. *De facto,* Pangerman politicians intend by this proposal to weaken non-German minorities, not to satisfy their national aspirations.

The delimitation of ethnographic frontiers will be governed by the parliamentary and democratic principle. For example, in restored Poland and Bohemia there will be German minorities; in Bohemia these minorities will be considerable; but the number of the German population in free Poland and free Bohemia will be far smaller than the number of Poles and Czechs in Polish and Czech territories at present under German and Austrian rule. Poles and Czechs are equal to the Germans in rights and worth; the Germans are not superior to them, and it is therefore more equitable than the present condition that there should be in Poland and Bohemia German minorities that will be smaller than the present Slav bodies oppressed by the Germans.

It should also be remarked that we lack at present reliable statistics of nationality. Ruling nations have used pressure of all kinds to diminish the number of the oppressed, using arbitrary, inexact language and national criteria (as, for instance, the "Umgangs-Sprache," language of intercourse, and the like). To gather careful demographic statistics is a trying need, not merely of history and science in general, but especially of politics.

The settlement of ethnographic boundaries after the storm of war will possibly be provisional in some cases;

as soon as the nations quiet down and accept the principle of self-determination, a rectification of ethnographic boundaries and minorities will be carried out without excitement and with due consideration of all questions involved.

12. EVERY NATIONAL QUESTION A SPECIAL PROBLEM

22. Every national question is an independent, peculiar problem, requiring the knowledge of existing conditions. One cannot sufficiently emphasize this rule of procedure. Justice to other nations requires knowledge of their problems, and precisely in this respect there is too little real knowledge of the language and nationality questions among the politicians and statesmen of Europe.

The contents of national controversies are very intricate. In some cases the language question plays the principal part; elsewhere the political problem is the main one, but both may be combined; the Czechs, for instance, carry on a language fight, but also a political fight to reclaim their historical right to an independent state. The Poles also appeal not merely to the ethnographic principle but also to their historical right; as against that, the Irish have practically no language question; their fight is more religious, social, and political. Elsewhere economic questions are in the forefront.

Nationality is expressed not merely through language, but through the entire culture—science and philosophy, jurisprudence and politics, morality and religion, art and technical science; custom and manners vary according to nationalities. For that reason national characteristics are felt and determined unequally. Not all nations are equally enlightened and determined to defend their nationality

and its cultural contents against another nationality;
therefore, for instance, the Bolsheviks propose the principle that the degree of development and civilization, or
backwardness, as the case may be, does not diminish the
right to self-determination. In view of the intricacy of
the problem, it may be said that there are as many
national questions as there are nationalities; there is no
single rule of dealing with all national questions.

13. MARXISM AND NATIONALITY

23. The Social Democracy, based upon Marxism, was
unable to understand and correctly judge this war: the
Marxist historical (economic) materialism does not possess true psychology, is unable to see and appreciate
properly individual and social forces which cannot be
reduced to the so-called economic conditions. Marxists,
therefore, do not realize that nationality—the national
idea and principle—constitutes an independent political
force alongside economic interest; neither are they able
to appreciate the religious and other forces. The reduc-
tion of all political phenomena to the economic interest
is a psychological impossibility.

This is true, of course, above all, of German Marxists.
Marx himself, before and even after the year 1848,
looked upon nationality in the same light as all the German radicals and liberals of that time; then the struggle
was for liberal reforms and for revolution against absolutism; there did not exist at that period a national question in Germany, just as there was none in England and
France. But in Austria and Prussia and Turkey (in the
Balkans) the liberal and democratic movement was at
the same time national. Marx based his theories on his

experiences in Germany, France, and England; at that time, just as did the German radicals, he judged national movements by the degree in which they were revolutionary. Being ignorant of national movements and aims he speaks of them, particularly of the smaller Slav nations, quite uncritically, in fact in a surprisingly superficial way. He gave his recognition to the Magyars, because they were against Austria and against Prussia; like all other liberals, radicals, and socialists, Marx saw in Russia the quintessence of absolutism; therefore, he gave his recognition to the Poles also, in the same way as did the other liberals of his day. But all these Polonophiles failed to see the Poles of Prussia; they saw only those of Russia.

Later on, when he formulated and elaborated his historical materialism, Marx condemned nationalism, as he condemns all other "ideologies," and he identified nationality with the State, and the State is to him only the greedy violence of the wealthy classes oppressing and exploiting the working people.

That the ideas of Marx on the question of nationality are uncritical and incorrect, and his judgments of the individual nations irrelevant and unjust, is today sufficiently evident; Marx is wrong, even if we accept his materialism. For that reason his followers in all the nationally mixed countries recognized the principle of nationality as an independent political factor alongside the economic factor—the French, Italian, Polish, Czech, and Jugoslav Marxist Socialists are also nationalists. The German socialists are not nationalists in theory, but they are so in practice, especially in Austria; in this war they (the majority) even joined the Pangermans. In England and America the national questions of the Euro-

pean continent are little understood. The same is true of
the Russians, who are acquainted at home only with
official nationalism which was working for the Russifica-
tion of the other races. In fact all of them rejected nationalism as chauvinism.[8]

From the analysis of the idea of nationality as given
above, it is evident that nationality and language, given
by nature and history, cannot be reduced either to the
economic or to the political factor—nationality is an
independent social force. Analysis makes it also evident
that socialism cannot reject nationality: a nation subju-
gated politically is exploited economically, socially—the
democratic program of liberty, equality, and fraternity
is at the same time a political, social, national, religious
program. Therefore socialism and nationalism develop
simultaneously and on the same ethical and humanitarian
foundation.

24. Lack of understanding of the principles of nationality leads many Marxists to an incorrect interpretation
of the war.

The favored phrase of the Marxists is that the present
war is a capitalistic war. But capital being on both warring sides, how then did it become the motive of the
war? The Germans declare that Russia started the war,
and here the German Marxists get into a very queer
position when they claim with William and his chancellors that Serbia and Russia, countries that are not capitalistic, or only half so, were responsible for the war.
That would really give us an agrarian aggression and

---

8. The Russian Social Revolutionist and former minister Czernov
wrote a pamphlet of some merit on the erroneous ideas of Marx as to
nationality; I called attention to this matter long ago in my book on
Marxism.

capitalistic defense. Of course the situation is complicated by the alliance of Russia with capitalistic France, and the accession of capitalistic England and America.

By their explanation the Marxists get into a peculiar position for this reason also, that they themselves accept and support capitalism to a certain extent, rejecting only its exploitation. They recognize its economic productiveness and its superiority to the agrarian and other degrees of economic development.

Another variation of the explanations given by the Marxists is this: the war arose out of imperialistic capitalism. The Marxists say that imperialism grows out of the modern industrial capitalism: industry needs markets, raw materials, and the like, therefore it subjugates colonies and agricultural countries.

The German, English, and French industrialism and capitalism have managed to harmonize their interest for quite a long while, since 1871; on several occasions disputes threatening war were peacefully settled (Morocco, etc.). Only a few months before the war Germany concluded a very advantageous agreement with England and the other colonial states; why then did the war break out so suddenly? Industrialism and capitalism do not suffice to explain that. As far as imperialism is concerned, it has already been said that the term is used very ambiguously; the German imperialism does no doubt play a decisive role in the war, but it is not only capitalistic and industrial; it arose long before Germany became a capitalistic and industrial country. As far as colonial imperialism is concerned, it is sufficient to call attention to the fact that the occupation of the colonies has preceded by centuries modern industrialism and capitalism. Besides, it is easy to prove that the foundation of colonies had other than merely industrial and capitalistic motives. Even during this war German economists and politicians were demonstrating that colonies did not pay, that on the contrary Germany had to make up an annual deficit for her colonies; and comparisons of world-trade figures show that Germany exported to England and imported materials from England for her industry to an amount forty times as great as the business done with her own colonies. The Marxists give credit to the shrewdness of merchants and capitalists for being rather sharp at sums and they ascribe to them an unmilitary spirit— and suddenly these merchants are accused of being more anxious for war than Mars himself, and of being fools in addition!

All these Marxist explanations of the war are just as one-sided and uncritical as the entire economic materialism and its philosophy of history, and therefore the official Marxist philosophy of this war is insufficient.

No one denies that economic interests play a great part in this war. We have become acquainted with Pangermanism, and know that its exponents emphasize Germany's need for soil, raw material, cheap labor, and so on. Perhaps every war was caused by a desire for material gain (*bonna terra, mali vicini*—I read in a medieval chronicle), but the question is, whether economic interests in any war, especially in this war, are the only decisive motives.

Their materialistic view of life brought the Marxists in this war into a compromising association with the Pangermanists; members of the German majority socialists, Lentch, Renner (the Austro-German socialistic leader), and others cannot be distinguished from Pangermanists. It would not, however, be fair, if I did not recall the author of *J'accuse*, who realized the situation very early; and now Kautsky and Bernstein criticize very effectively the Marxist one-sided explanation of the war. In Russia Plechanov did not succumb to the war cries of the one-sided Bolshevism.

III. THE EASTERN QUESTION

14. THE PROGRAM OF THE ALLIES PRIMARILY FOR THE REORGANIZATION OF EASTERN EUROPE

25. All European States were disturbed by the social question, but that did not lead to serious international complications, whereas the national struggles troubled and upset the whole of international relations. In the West the only acute national questions were the problems of the Danes in Schleswig, and of Alsace-Lorraine. The Irish question is not a national question (not in the sense in which, for instance, the Polish or the Czecho-Slovak questions are national). The dispute between the Walloons and the Flemings in Belgium has never been acute, as this war has demonstrated, for the Flemings defended Belgium against Germany with a determination equal to that of the Walloons, and their representatives opposed separation from the Walloons; but in the East there have existed quite a number of acute national disputes, more serious than any of those in the West; the question of the Poles, Czecho-Slovaks, and Jugoslavs (Serbo-Croatians, Slovenes), the Ukrainian question in Galicia and Hungary, the Roumanian, the Italian, Macedonian, Albanian and Greek questions. In Russia the

most acute national problems were the Polish and Finnish; but since the war, national aspirations have been strengthened in Lithuania, among the Letts and Esthonians, and in the Caucasus and the East. A unique question is the Jewish question (in all lands).

This state of things was known before the war to those who paid some deeper attention to political questions, the evidence of it being found in the many publications of all these national issues. The Great Powers, some being directly interested, and others from diplomatic connivance, minimized these struggles and declared them to be "internal affairs." The war, however, compelled official Europe to take heed of the true condition, namely, that the zone from the Baltic Sea to the Adriatic, the Aegean and Black Seas, which includes Prussia, Austria-Hungary, the Balkans, and Western Russia, is a territory of unsettled national problems and struggles. The war is a bloody object-lesson for the world, teaching that the principal problem of the war and of the future peace is the political reconstruction of Eastern Europe on a national basis. The program indicated in the note of the Allies addressed to President Wilson, his own program, and all other programs, naturally refer to the situation in the East of Europe, the zone of the small nations, and to Russia. The now current phrase *Reconstruction,* means reconstruction in the East. For England, France, and Italy reconstruction means something quite different from what it means for the future Poland, Czecho-Slovakia, Roumania. In the East there must be a readjustment of political boundaries; new States and governments are to be organized; the greater part of Europe is to be politically reshaped.

26. We maintain that every national question is a complicated, special problem. Therefore it would require a detailed historical exposition and analysis of the national condition of Germany-Prussia, Austria-Hungary, Balkan-Turkey, and Russia to make clear the rich contents of the various national problems, and to explain why the national questions are most acute in these States. Here I can only set down the main facts and the leading principles.

It has already been noted that Germany, and especially Prussia, germanized a large part of the Slavs. From the Elbe and Saale the Germans pressed constantly toward the Slav East, until they succeeded in dismembering Poland, for it was the Prussian king, Frederick the Great, who instigated the partition of that country. Bismarck formulated the leading aims of Prussian-German politics when he declared the Province of Posen (the part of Poland held by Germany) to be incomparably more important for the Germans than Alsace-Lorraine. The policy of Berlin and the voice of influential German publicists and politicians prove that the push toward the East is still considered by Germany as her traditional aim.

The Hapsburgs, who ruled long over Germany, carried out German policies, and threatened equally the Slav East and South; they oppressed the Czechs and Slovaks, annexed a large part of Poland, pressed against the Jugoslavs, Roumanians, and Italians. The Germans, like the Mongolian Magyars, effected a reconciliation with the traditional enemy of Christianity, Turkey, against the Slavs. In this war prussianized Germany, Austria-Hungary, and Turkey formed a league against Europe

—an anti-national, undemocratic, dynastic, aggressive league.

The acuteness of the nationality question in Prussia, Austria-Hungary, Turkey (the Balkans)—and the same has been true, to a large extent, of Russia also—lies in this, that these States oppress nations and national minorities that are self-conscious and enlightened, nations that formerly enjoyed political independence, or nations, parts of which now constitute independent States. Alsace-Lorraine, even while it was connected with the old empire, was in reality an independent country, and received from France French culture; the Danish minority in Schleswig has likewise been independent, and its degree of cultural development is as high as that of the Germans. Poland, too, has been independent; it was divided in a treacherous manner, and oppressed, although a considerable part of the nation, as far as culture is concerned, was highly developed. The Czechs and Slovaks had likewise been independent; the Czechs *de jure* still are independent, and their culture is in no manner inferior to that of the Germans; neither are the Slovaks at a lower degree of cultural development than the Magyars who oppress them. The same is true of the Serbians and Croatians; Serbia and Montenegro are independent, and the Jugoslavs, held down by Austria and Hungary, naturally look to them for the realization of their ideal; Croatia has maintained a certain degree of independence, and for that reason feels Magyar oppression the more. The situation of the Roumanians and the Italians is similar.

The nations of the Balkans have only in recent years freed themselves from the barbarous yoke of the Turks, and have not yet quieted down. Turkey still holds a part of the Greeks in subjection, and interferes, to the detriment of the Balkans. In the national questions of the Balkans the cultural and political influence of Byzantium still plays a considerable part.

If we compare with these national questions the national questions of the West, we perceive a great difference. In the first place, the West has very few national disputes, the only pressing question in the West being Alsace-Lorraine; but in the East there are at least nine acute questions. In the West disputes turn on relatively smaller minorities (140,000 Danes, 210,000 French), whereas, in the East entire nations of a considerable size are at stake (Poles, 20 million; Czecho-Slovaks, 10 million; Jugoslavs, 10 million; Roumanians, 10 million, etc.).

As far as the dispute between Germany and France is concerned, it is not altogether national. Between the two nations and States the dispute has raged for centuries about a comparatively insignificant territory, and less than two million people. The dispute all along turned on the question of power, not of nationality, which latter was the case between the Germans and the smaller Slav States; the aggressive German colonization is aimed against the East. Therefore we may say once more that in the West there really were no national disputes, and that the West in general, as has been explained, differs politically and nationally from the East, and especially from that peculiar central zone of smaller nations between the Germans and the Russians.

The war arose from a dispute over little Serbia—the Austro-Hungarian Great Power, 51 million people against 4½, declared that its existence was endangered. Today the war is waged between great and very great

States, but the racial composition of the large Eastern
States turns the question of power into the question of
the small nations.

15. THE DISMEMBERMENT OF AUSTRIA-HUNGARY AS THE PRINCIPAL AIM OF THE WAR: "THE IDEA OF THE AUSTRIAN STATE"

27. Austria-Hungary, composed of nine nations, is
altogether an artificial State; as a leader of the Austrian
Germans, von Plenner, Jr., once expressed it, it is a
State composed of fairly large and civilized nations, held
in subjection by the dynasty and the German Magyar
minority. If the principle that nations are entitled to self-
determination is meant in earnest, Austria-Hungary is
politically and morally condemned, for since the latter
part of the eighteenth century all Austro-Hungarian nations have been striving to attain freedom and independence. Austria is a medieval survival. As against modern
democracy and nationality Austria represents the old
dynastic State; Dr. Seidler, the Austrian Prime Minister,
in rejecting the right of nations to self-determination,
expressed only what had been expressed in 1848 by the
Austrian bishops and what has been put in practice by
Vienna at all times. Of course, the dynasty had to lean
on some nationality (German-Magyar), but it used its
nations against one another (*Divide et Impera*). Against
its nations Austria sets the dynasty by the grace of God
and the army; against democracy it sets its aristocracy,
an aristocracy peculiarly selfish and narrow-minded—as
has been said, a kind of an East Indian exploiting company. The Habsburgs, who have been for centuries
German Emperors, appropriated to their use the me-

dieval imperialistic idea, and still employ it, even though they have given up formally the German Imperial crown. They were devoted servants of the Church, misusing religion for their family interests. The Habsburgs accomplished the anti-Reformation with the help of dragoons and Jesuits: *Geistesmörder* was the name given to the régime of Metternich and Bach by one of the greatest German-Austrian poets. The Pope himself admitted recently that he worked for the preservation of the last great Catholic State. Clericalism in practice directs Habsburg imperialism, which lately was aimed at the Greek Orthodox Churches of Russia and of the Balkans. (This traditional task of Austria was well pointed out in a pamphlet written by the German theologian, Erhart.) The whole régime of Francis Joseph had its policy based on this clerical imperialism; Francis Ferdinand with his "Gross-Oesterreich" differed only on the point of tactics, which his adherents declared to be firm determination.

Palacký, who, in 1846, was the first man to set up for Austria the program of a free federation of nations, attempted, as late as 1865, to discover "the Idea of the Austrian State"; it was to be an Austria just to its nations. This is the Austria that Palacký had in mind when he declared in 1848 that Austria would have to be created over again if it did not exist. But the introduction of Dualism in 1867 taught Palacký that one could not expect justice from Austria. Czech statesmen of more recent days have long tried to look upon Austria as Palacký did in 1865, but Austria went on its fateful road. The Triple Alliance and the occupation of Bosnia-Herzegovina made of it a submissive German vanguard in the East; its moral baseness was revealed by the diplomatic intrigues during Aehrenthal's chancellorship and by the Zagreb (Agram) and Friedjung trials. The last Balkan Wars, and finally this war, were merely the culmination of Austro-German politics. Mazzini, after the war of 1866, made a correct diagnosis of Austria when he said that the downfall of Turkey would be followed by the downfall of Austria—both these political anomalies have stood together and are falling together.

That Austria is something abnormal is admitted even by these German statesmen who are now busy figuring how to keep Austria alive: Renner, Pernersdorfer, Bahr, Mueller, and others, who admit that Austria, if it is to exist longer, must be transformed. Vain attempts—all these German plans aim to maintain the German-Magyar hegemony, even though they would like to reach their goal in a cleverer and more decent manner.[1]

Austria is, in all its substance—its history, geography, and ethnography—a denial of the modern State and nationality. From its very foundation it had no *raison d'être* of its own, being an outpost of Germany and serving that empire; it is a mere annex to Germany even today. By its medieval dynastic theocratism it is the denial of democracy and nationality. Some Pangermans quite properly condemn the national amorphism and lack of character of Vienna (to quote Mueller as a recent example).

28. Count Czernin emphasizes the peculiar vitality and strength of Austria-Hungary. We have already made

---

1. In this respect the program of the German Socialists Renner and Bauer shows no essential difference from the Pangerman program. Renner accepts Naumann's Central Europe and national autonomy, as he and Bauer explain it, merely as a concession for the purpose of preserving Austria-Hungary and her German character.

it plain that Austria is not a natural federation of nations, but that it is kept alive through Jesuitism and
blood and iron; the Pope himself, a friend of Austria,
called the late Emperor for his terrorism during the
war "the bloodthirsty sovereign." Gladstone's condemnation of Austria is wholly justified. But the fact is, that
in the present war Austria gave no proof of its vitality;
it was twice defeated by Russia; it was defeated even by
the small despised Serbia, and only Germany saved it
from downfall. The war demonstrated the complete in-
efficiency, entire degeneration of the leading archdukes
and aristocrats, and the same qualities are exhibited by
the new emperor and his chancellors who cannot say a
single manly word, but only repeat phrases with the usual
stupid cleverness. Emperor Charles is under the influence
of the Clericals; without experience, without political
ideas, without a will for modern policy, he naturally
leans upon the ancient and sole idea of his dynasty. In
the affair of his letter to Prince Sixtus, Emperor Charles
showed anew the substance of Austria's policies—lying.[2]

The true state of things has manifested itself in this
war. The Czecho-Slovaks, Jugoslavs, Ukrainians, Italians, Roumanians, and very soon the Poles also, refused

2. Emperor Charles wrote for the benefit of the President of the
French Republic, in the evident hope that the French would not see
through the trickiness of himself and his advisers; his real plan was
expressed in another letter, addressed to Ferdinand of Roumania; here
he emphasized the idea that kings must now hold together to defend
monarchism against the democratic movements.

These principles agree literally with the aims which Emperor William
pursued, just as Bismarck and Count Czernin, the friend and adviser
of Charles, made William's principles his own. I gave a report of a
memorandum of Count Czernin, written for Francis Ferdinand, in which
he emphasizes the importance of William's plans to maintain monarchism
by a close union of the monarchs; in that memorandum emphasis also
is laid upon the German character of Austria-Hungary and its friendship with Germany. (*See* the article in Plekhanov's *Edinstvo* of June
9, 1917, reprinted in the *Christian Science Monitor*.)

obedience and took a stand against Austria—60,000 executions and the assistance of Germany upheld the Habsburgs for a while. Even the Magyars are against Austria, and among the Germans the Pangermans have been the greatest radicals in demanding the annexation of Austria to Germany. Pangermans reconciled themselves during the war to Austria, but their only reason is, that Austria carries out unconditionally the task assigned to her by Bismarck and Lagarde, as one of the leaders (deputy Iro) says plainly. Europe and America have the choice between a degenerate dynasty and the liberty of nine nations, for even the Germans and Magyars will reach a higher degree of political morality if they are compelled to give up the exploitation of other nations and their subserviency to a reactionary dynasty. Austria has been on the downgrade for a long time; step by step it has had to surrender parts of its territory (Swiss, Belgian, Italian); Prussia thrust it out of Germany, and the final internal dissolution began with the introduction of dualism. The dissolution of Austria is a natural and necessary historical process.

29. The Pangerman politicians of Austria plan to strengthen Austria by making it smaller. To give up Trentino to Italy, to surrender, if necessary, Bukovina, a part, or even the whole, of Galicia, would not, according to their scheme, make Austria weaker; it would cease to be in opposition to Italy, Poland would be under Austrian and German influence, and a territorial indemnity would be found for ceded territory in the Balkans and in Russia (Ukraina!). The restoration of the small, weakened Serbia would not, for some time, be in the way of the plan to unify the Jugoslavs under Austria,

and in that way to occupy the Balkans. These plans are
purely Pangermanist. The Pangermans, even Schoenerer
himself, have long ago demanded the separation of
Galicia and Dalmatia—which would give the Germans
a secure majority in the parliament against the Czechs,
who are the greatest and the most powerful obstacle to
the Pangerman plans.

30. Many imagine that Austria was driven into the
war by Germany against its will, and that after the war
it will be opposed to Germany. That is a misreading of
history; Austria from its inception served the German
ideal; the German publicists of Austria (for instance,
the above-quoted Mueller) understand that very well—
a little freedom conceded to the Slavs will not hinder
Germanization through ideas. Germanization is possible
even by means of the Slav tongues; and the rivalry with
Prussia, as we have shown, actually strengthened the
German ideal in Prussia and in Austria, until Bismarck
finally found the definite formula for the organization
of Pangerman aggression.

In addition to that, the Magyars have delivered themselves to Germany hand and foot, as is constantly declared not merely by Tisza but also by Andrássy, Karolyi,
and all the others. Vienna and Budapest will not be anti-
German. Neither are the speculations based on the differences of church and religion well founded. Germany
occupied Austria politically, the Catholics in Germany
will occupy her ecclesiastically; they well know that Austrian Catholicism is a mire—it was termed so expressly
by the Catholic organ of Cologne—but the Jesuits of
Cologne and Rome do not mind it; on the contrary, that
will make Vienna the more subservient and the Centrum

in Germany will get the political leadership of the Austrian weaklings. The Prussia of Frederick and Bismarck is no whit better, as far as Jesuitism goes, than the Centrum at Vienna. The policy of Austria, aiming only to preserve the dynastic prestige, is always contented with appearances; Berlin very cleverly complies with Vienna's wishes and does not worry if the Habsburgs maintain the appearance of independence and even primacy. It does not, for instance, matter to Berlin that Vienna proceeds in a different manner in the Polish question; Berlin does not care that Austrian agents, especially in America and England, intimate that Austria is opposed to Berlin, that it was dragged into the war, that it has had enough of war, etc.; in reality Austria is not opposed to Berlin, but accepts all that Berlin considers necessary. And if Vienna sometimes really goes its own way, even that does not bother Berlin in the end—Berlin and Vienna are like Siamese twins. Their cooperation in the main direction is best illustrated by this war: the war was provoked by Austria and its false anti-Serbian and anti-Slav policy; Germany used the opportunity to give her ally *carte blanche,* and in this way, being well prepared and desirous of war, she tried to conceal her complicity under the guise of faithfulness to her ally.[3]

31. The Austrophiles defend Austria by pointing spe-

---

3. I formulated this judgment of Austrian Catholicism years ago in a lecture given in Boston (1907). I repeat: the dynasty and the State are maintained by these powers, and are without that religious vitality which Catholicism has in those countries where, as in America, for instance, it stands on its own feet. It is an interesting fact in general that Catholicism is strong in Protestant and liberal countries; it is dead where it is the *beatus possidens.* The severe judgment of the German Catholic journal is fully justified; Austrian Catholicism is characterized, for instance, by the fact that its chief dignitaries are aristocrats, and it is understood that the Emperor selects only such persons as suit him. "No; God is not an Austrian" (*Byron*).

cifically to the Czechs and claiming that they reached
under Austria that high degree of culture which everywhere is recognized with admiration. We reached that
culture through our own initiative and strength, nay, in
spite of Austria; Vienna never favored our nation nor
any of her other nations; it was only when its intrigues
and oppression failed that at most it ceased for a time
to place obstacles in our way. Already in the Middle
Ages Bohemia was one of the most highly developed
countries. After the disaster caused by the Austrian anti-
Reformation, the Czech nation recovered in spite of all
Austria opposition, and continued in its traditions; and
if Vienna did not in recent times block the economic
development of the Czech lands as it used to formerly,
it was moved by financial reasons; the dynasty needs
great sums of money for the maintenance of the army
and bureaucracy, which laterly have become the refuge
of the aristocracy. Therefore it permits the Czech nation
to develop economically in the interest of the machinery
of the State, thereby serving in the first place the interests of the dynasty.

32. Some friends of Austria in the West also use the
argument that we are fighting Germany and its Prussian
militarism, and that Germany, therefore, must not be
strengthened by being permitted to annex the German
provinces of Austria. This is a problem in arithmetic:
is 7 greater than 50? Heretofore Germany had at its
disposal the whole of Austria—51 million people;
through the dismemberment of Austria-Hungary it would
get only the German part of it—only 7 or 8 million
people. (The German minorities in the Czech lands, in
Hungary, and elsewhere would not become a part of
Germany.) It is, of course, up to the Habsburgs, whether

they will maintain their independence; most likely they will choose to follow the example of the Byzantine emperors; they may remain emperors even after they have lost their territorial empire. That would not matter to Berlin; on the contrary, Berlin would not have to pay any attention to its cries of *panem et circenses,* and it would no longer be disturbed by the claims of a rival capital. Austria is the strong, yet also the weak, spot of the German body. Without Austria and its non-German nations Germany would be compelled to live like all the other nations—by its own strength. The dismemberment of Austria will be the greatest blow to Prussianized Germany. This should be clear to everyone, particularly since the military and political downfall of Russia. A strong Russia was a powerful military and political support to the Western nations. With its military and economic strength weakened, Russia could easily become the prey of Germany, unless Austria-Hungary is dismembered. By the dismemberment of Austria, Russia will be best protected, having lost its principal enemy, and having ceased to share common boundaries with Germany.

33. It is necessary to say a few words about the Magyars and their State.

Today the Magyars—especially in the West—still thrive politically on the revolution of 1848 and on Kossuth, although even then the Magyars oppressed the other nations of Hungary. This was well perceived by Cavour in his characterization of the Magyars, when he said that they fought for their own liberty but would not allow liberty to others. The Magyars lack a deeper culture. The Magyar people are in no respect superior to the Slovaks; quite the contrary is evident from the fact that the Magyar language has appropriated from the Slovak quite a number of terms pertaining to agriculture, administration, and general culture.

The Magyars are an aristocratic nation, where a numerous nobility and landed gentry making common cause with the capitalistic interest maintain themselves in power through violence. This exploiting Junker class keeps the foreign countries in ignorance as to the true state of affairs. Ignorance of the Magyar language and the impossibility of any real control on the part of the West enable the Magyars to practice oligarchy, absolutism, and a Magyarizing imperialism.

They clothe this absolutism with a pretended respectability by terming it "the idea of the Hungarian State"; in this the Magyars are at one with the German Junkers upholding the idea of the Prussian State. Even the founder of the Hungarian State, St. Stephen, declared that a state like Hungary would be imperfect if resting only on one nation. The political views of nations which practice oppression are everywhere and always the same; among the Prussians, Austrians, Magyars, and Turks there is indeed harmony in spirit.

The Magyars turn all their energies against the Slovaks, Ruthenians, Jugoslavs and Roumanians; their anti-Slavic baiting, which always found willing champions, especially in the Viennese press, is largely responsible for this war.

16. PRUSSIAN GERMANY: THE CULTURE OF EXTERNAL ORDER AND MILITARISTIC MATERIALISM

34. Prussia, as we have pointed out, has much in com-

mon with Austria in its origin and in the eastern aims of its policy and its tactics, even though there are considerable differences of temperament and character between the Germans of Prussia (Northern Germans) and those of Austria, who are, to a considerable extent, under the influence of the other nations of Austria-Hungary and who also differ racially.

Prussia today is more nationally unified; to maintain national unity by all means is the principal point of the Pangerman program, and the weakness of Austria and Russia, because of their national diversity, is pointed out. For that reason the Pangermans demand forcible Germanization, colonization, and wholesale emigration of non-German elements. Prussia is, after Austria and Russia, the most nationally mixed country; thus ethnography bears testimony to the fact that Prussia was built up by violence. The Prussians themselves are a Germanized nation, related to the Lithuanians; there are also many Germanized Slavs in present Prussia. According to Bismarck, it is a crossing of a female race (Slavs) and a male race (Prussian-German).

From the Pangerman plans, from political maxims enunciated by men like Bismarck, and now from the whole war and peace maneuvers of Germany and Austria, it is evident that the object of the German aggression is the East (*Drang nach Osten*). The first and principal point of the German eastern policy is to hold Austria-Hungary; Austria is to Germany a bridge, as the title of a Pangerman pamphlet has it—the bridge to the Balkans and Turkey, and therefore to Asia and Africa. Germany in union with Austria presses into Russia; the nominal freedom of the Baltic provinces, of Russian Poland and the Ukraine, is a temporary expedient. Belgium, Alsace-Lorraine, and the West in general, have, as the world situation stands today, a much smaller importance for the Germans, if they succeed in winning the East; if they rule the East they will easily settle the bill against France and England, and later even against the United States.

35. In the course of the war the French, English, and Americans, have realized the true condition of affairs. The Italians have for a long time been against Austria, and for that reason they take such an emphatic stand against Prussian militarism.

Prussian militarism leads us to the analysis of the whole Prussian question. In Germany this question is looked upon as meaning that the Prussian diet must be made more democratic, and the existence of political differences between Eastern and Western Germany (Prussian Junkers) is admitted; but there is a wider and deeper Prussian problem—the problem formulated by Pangermanism and its philosophers, Lagarde, von Hartmann, and others, the problem of the difference between the Prussian and southern German spirit, the problem of the right of Prussia to lead Germany, and actually to Prussianize Germany. The difference is brought out in the motto: "Goethe or Bismarck?" The answer usually given is that there exists a difference, but that it is insignificant, and that as far as any exists, it tends to increase the content of German culture; but right now during the war some Austrian and Prussian Germans search their conscience, and reach the conclusion that Prussian Germandom has a clear title to stand alongside Austrian Germandom, and emphasis is laid on the organic synthesis of the two directions of the German national spirit.

One does not like to pass a summary judgment upon

such a complicated subject without a lengthy reasoning. While pointing to my former statements I will give here with all proper reserve my opinion, an opinion which, it seems to me, is well founded. I will not go into racial problems, namely, how far the Prussians of today possess the qualities of the original Prussians, whom German historians themselves declared to be a brave and cruel race. Neither is it practicable to investigate how much Slav blood there is in the Prussians and Germans. This analysis would make it necessary to go into the question of how far the Southern (and Western) Germans are racially mixed, for these also are not purely German (Celtic, Slav, Mongolian, and other admixtures). Here it must suffice to speak of the Prussian political program. I then reject the Prussian worship of the State, and specifically the Prussian monarchism; I reject the idea of the Prussian kingship, according to which the dynasty is looked upon as a divine revelation. I reject the Prussian denial of parliamentarism, its apotheosis of war, the worship of militarism and militaristic bureaucratism. This Prussianism is deeply rooted; Sombart is the spokesman of thousands of educated Germans, both when he sees the substance of German thought in the faculty of finding union with the divinity even here on earth and when he sees in militarism the most perfect union of Weimar with Potsdam ("he is the Faust, Zarathustra and Beethoven in the trenches"). Sombart's divinity, of course, is the fetish of his pedantic historical materialism.

Bismarck shows what Prussianism is politically; his life really consisted in safeguarding the Prussian monarchism against revolution, against socialism and democracy, and a part of this Bismarck is in every German,

even in Messrs. Scheidemann and David; these very
socialists who have become reconciled even to monarchism, indicate the degree to which Germans have become
accustomed to Prussian militarism and monarchism; but
the tragedy of Bismarck's life and his policy lies in this,
that in the end he rebelled against William in opposition
to his own idea; Bismarck knew and saw what weak and
vain representatives of his idea he defended; he un-
veiled the monarchical Isis. . . . In this fatal contradiction (Bismarck played with Lassalle, but Lassalle also
played with Bismarck) Bismarck systematized the Prussian political Jesuitism; he, the foe of Austrian Jesuitism
and its narrowness. Those who analyze deeper psychologically cannot be deceived by Bismarck's tactics, using
against the old-style diplomacy the bluff of robust half-
truth. Bismarck defended a lost position, and he understood that it was lost, and yet he practiced conscientiously
the policy of "blood and iron," from which, as we know
from Busch, he never derived any joy or satisfaction;
and this Bismarck, and men like Treitschke, carried out
the synthesis of Weimar with Potsdam; Treitschke declared morality to be the endowment of small men
undertaking small things, whereas the State must carry
out great things. This internal contradiction of Bismarck
is involved in the very conception and substance of the
Prussian State; a State by God's grace whose dynasts
are supposed to be the prophets of God, is in all its
substance conservative, legitimist; but imperialistic aggressiveness compelled the Prussian king by irony and
trickery to absorb his neighboring dynasts, who also
ruled by God's grace (Prussia arose by the absorption
of more than a hundred dynasties), and drove him to
come to terms with socialism and revolution.

Right here we put our finger on Prussian materialism;
just because a state has at its disposal an effective army
and can mobilize masses does not make it great, unless
all its endeavors are honest and generous. Prussian politics never were honest and generous (see, for example, the
dishonorable peace with revolutionary Russia: William
makes agreements with Trotzky—the super-legitimate
monarch with a revolutionist, and, what is more, a Jew,
who in William's army could not be promoted to be an
officer. In Prussia the nationalities are suppressed, but in
Belgium the Prussians fostered the Flemings, etc.). The
Prussians lack that generosity which the French possess,
and the Germans do not have that *naïveté* and sincerity
that characterizes Englishmen and Americans. The Prussian is on guard all the time and against all.

36. The Germans advance the claim to primacy by pointing to their philosophy and science, and emphasize the
utilization of science in all administrative and military
affairs, in political economy and commerce. German
science, it is true, is efficient, but it is not free, it is a part
of the official system. German universities are intellectual
barracks. German philosophy is deep, but much of its
depth forced, artificially produced by the lack of liberty;
it is but the modernization of scholastics—the whole
political aim set out in advance is proved and applied by
all sorts of *ex post* arguments. German philosophy, as
far as it is not based on specialized science, is nothing but
Sunday sermons for the academic youth, the future officials of the church and state. Look at the German literature in the field of jurisprudence, especially in the science
of state and politics, and see how much brainwork is employed there for the advance of theocratic absolutism,
what special legal categories are devised for a peculiar

monarchical right, of a special monarchical "office," etc., while the matter really is very simple—judged from a higher degree of enlightenment and education. Monarchist absolutism is simply immoral. Even during this war German jurists and philosophers argue for the superiority of the Prussian-German state and its administration over the English and Western systems in general. There is nothing so absurd but that the German professors cannot cleverly defend it. I am sorry that even such a man as Toennies stoops to this; according to him the West has gone in theory beyond the medieval theocratism, and therefore it looks upon the State from a utilitarian point of view, for this is what democracy means to him; evidently the Prussians can stand theocratic tsarism, and so it is no accident that Treitschke gave his recognition to Russian tsarism, and that the Hohenzollerns and Bismarck have been so long and so intimately devoted to old Russia. Now they are in alliance with Turkish theocratism and are its defenders.

37. German scholastics is at its best in theology, namely, in the so-called modern theology; in the Prussian theocratic system the State has the largest share, and therefore its theology is nothing but politics in ecclesiastical and religious guise. Ludwig Feuerbach and his criticism of theology is in substance a criticism of Prussianism.

German scholastics arose in the same way as Jesuitism in the Catholic Church. Besides, the Hohenzollerns must have a regard to the Centrum and the Catholics, and in their rivalry with Austria they employed the methods of Viennese Jesuitism. Prussia-Germany absorbed Austria, but incidentally it swallowed a portion of Austrianism and now it absorbs and swallows even Mohammedanism. Prussia betrayed the Reformation: Prussia is secular

Jesuitism—in its endeavor to maintain medieval theocratism at all cost it follows the same methods as the Society of Jesus. In this respect Prussia spiritually leads Austria, and this is its great crime; Pangerman publicists know Austria quite well; men like Treitschke, Lagarde, Lange, and others, know that Austria is a political misfit and a medieval mummy. The first generation of Pangermans was in favor of the disruption of Austria, but Bismarck and Lagarde established the tactics for using Austria for their own purposes. There are still men who see through Bismarckism, but they are few; only recently the Socialist minority are beginning to think more for themselves. Bismarck himself was under no misconception of the real situation—hence his attempt at the cultural fight against the Centrum and Rome; but Bismarck surrendered because he valued the Church and religion for their usefulness as a political weapon. How contemptuously he looked upon the Old Catholics! This flower of German Catholicism and Catholic theology meant nothing to him, because it did not have behind it the masses. Prussian monarchism today can only be a form of demagogy.

Jesuitism forms also the substance of Prussian militarism: brutal bravery united to trickiness—systematic violence employing lies, for lying is but a form of violence.[4]

---

4. William is responsible for the brutal exhortation to the Germans to employ the example of the Huns in their treatment of the Chinese. The Germans purposely try to terrorize the opposing armies and populations; the Russians also committed some inhuman deeds in Western Prussia, but the Russians do not pretend to be the most cultured nation; their army does not excel in discipline, and, moreover, they were retreating. The Germans committed barbarities quite consciously and systematically; therefore, in view of their discipline, the responsibility rests on their leaders. Had the leaders given humane commands the soldiers would have observed them; the Germans, it must be borne in mind, committed their barbarities while victoriously advancing.

If war, as a Prussian military expert said, is merely a different form of politics, then surely German militarism does not produce men of the type of Achilles but of Ulysses. Hence the absence of a truly great commander like Napoleon. All the Hindenburgs and their like are good, painstaking, and conscientious generals, but they do not possess the slightest spark of genius. It cannot be otherwise; the Germans have no great ideas, only the craftiness of a greedy aggressiveness. German diplomacy and its underground work in all countries is the natural ally of Prussian militarism.

38. All German culture, if one may venture into such a large generalization, is external. Germany's strength and weakness lie in its outward orderliness; organization everywhere, organization of organizations, superorganization; but the ultimate aim, dominion over all nations, is morally wrong. Prussian order, scientifically thought out, is a force, and the Germans, therefore, look upon themselves as "Herrenvolk"; but a little more or less culture, and especially of this superficial culture, gives them no right to dominate nations which develop in their own way. Various nations are at various stages of development; it is nowhere decreed that all nations must be equally educated at the same time; it is enough if they honestly work for their moral and intellectual improvement. Europe should be unified and unitary, but that does not mean that it should be uniform. On the contrary, development aims at variation, at individualization. The Germans, in spite of all their science, proved even in this war how shortsighted they can be. Though they were well prepared for war—in fact, they alone were prepared— they did not see how the war would develop. They under-

estimated Russia, overestimated Austria, failed to understand England and America, and were totally deceived as
to France, which they declared to be degenerate. Altogether, the Germans have in this war, and even in their
victories, proved themselves small. We acknowledge that
we are indebted for much to German literature, science,
and philosophy, and to German technique. But we also
derived much education from the French, English, Italians, Russians, and Scandinavians. The cultivation of
reason is only a part of true culture—here we could refer
also to German psychology and philosophy, but the official German science and the philosophy of the universities
serve exclusively the cult of reason, and thereby of materialistic Prussianism and of military and economic materialism. We reject, in the name of humanity and true
culture, the materialism and mechanism of Prussian militarism. One is reminded of the words of Herzen about
Djingis-Khan with telegraphs, steamers, and railroads,
with Carnot and Monge in his staff, with Mignet-Con-
greve rifles, under the leadership of Baty; the tactics of
Moltke, the diplomacy of Bismarck and his successors
down to Bismarck and William compel us to be critical of
the Germans and their culture; for that matter Moltke
himself well knew that the European nations could not
be fond of the Germans.

17. THE REORGANIZATION OF EASTERN EUROPE
AND RUSSIA

39. The difference between the West and Russia, as
far as nationality and politics are concerned, has already
been pointed out; in the West there are many nations and
States; Russia has many nations, but forms one State. On

a territory not larger though more densely populated, the West is a political organization of numerous and highly cultured old nations; it represents politically, economically, and culturally a more intensive organization, a more intensive employment of all cultural forces, whereas Russia is still at the stage of extensiveness. The West is an organization of autonomous national and State units, Russia has been a centralistic, absolutist organization. It was by the lack of decentralization that tsarism fell. For that reason also the revolution immediately proclaimed the autonomist war-cry of self-determination of nations, and the radical factions interpret the right of self-determination as the right to political separation; this program was bound to come up in a country so highly centralized by sheer force. In the West— what a variety of independent languages, nations, and States; in tsarist Russia, though with a population half that of the West—what a monotony of administration; and yet even the West is not sufficiently decentralized. Russia does not lack natural and historical variety of cultural forces, but tsarism was unable to stir up and organize these forces; that was the cause of its breakdown and disappearance. For that reason the revolution is still so negative, so lacking in constructive force. Tsarism did not prepare the Russians for administrative work.

From the national point of view Russia is a peculiar formation composed of many nations; a German author from one of the Baltic provinces published recently in Paris, under the name of Inorodec, a treatise on Russia, in which he enumerates 111 nationalities composing Russia, European and Asiatic. His purpose, like that of all Pangermanists, is to bring out the composite character of Russia and use it in the defence of the composite char-

acter of Austria-Hungary and Russia; but between Russia
on the one hand and Austria-Hungary and Prussia on
the other there is a great difference, as far as the question of nationality goes.

The great majority of the peoples of Russia are un-
educated and without national conscience; the Russians
themselves have not developed to the point of national
consciousness; the masses of the people have their religious viewpoint, and the *intelligentsia,* as far as it is
Socialistic, does not feel nationally. The watchword of
self-determination of nations is applied by the Russians
to their various parts; hence the birth of so many republics, or rather communes; and, therefore, the solution of
national and language questions in Russia is different
from the European solution.

Out of this great number of nations very few, and
those only in small part, extend across the frontiers into
other States, especially into the European States. In fact,
only the civilized nations in the West of Russia do so
(the Poles, Roumanians, a part of the Lithuanians and
Letts); the overwhelming majority of the Russian nations are united within the boundaries of the Empire; and
it must be noted that the nations of Russia are on the
whole small, fragmentary, and, in addition to that, un-
educated.

Russia for centuries pushed to the West, directly
against that zone of small nations into which the Germans pushed in an easterly direction; in that zone, Russia, Prussia, and Austria met and struggled for domination over these small nations. At the same time Russia
grew toward the East; that was the result of the pressure
from the Asiatics and of Russia's weakness as against the

West. In contrast with the Western nations, which pushed without exception toward East and South, Russia colonized first the North, and only later turned toward the East and South both in Europe and Asia.

The most acute national question has been the Polish, but this is not a question of nationality only, but also of politics and culture in general (Catholicism and Western culture). The same is true of the Finnish (Protestantism and racial difference). The Germans in Russia do not possess a continuous territory, they are colonists; their colonies, especially in the Baltic districts, date from the period of the knights of military orders. There are no German provinces in Russia; but there are Polish provinces in Prussia. If William, after the conclusion of the peace with Trotsky and Lenin, declared solemnly that the Baltic Germans might thereafter publicly call themselves Germans, that only proves that not even the war has cured the man of his talkativeness. The Baltic provinces are not German but Lithuanian, Lettish, and Esthonian, and a considerable part, perhaps the majority, of the German barons and burghers did not share the opinions of Schiemann and Rohrbach, but were reconciled to Russia, especially the official Russia, which allowed them to exploit the non-German population and the country very effectively. The non-German population of the Baltic provinces has frequently protested, through its spokesmen, against the German occupation and the design to settle German dynasts there.

40. In the Ukrainian problem we must carefully distinguish the question of language and nationality from the political question. The point lies in this: Are the

Ukrainians a separate nation or a Russian tribe? Is the Ukrainian language a separate language or a Russian dialect? Even the philologists (Slavic) are divided on this question. Following the analogy of other nations, however, we may say that the Ukrainians, even granting that their tongue is merely a dialect of the Russian—and that is my opinion—may separate themselves from the Russians on other grounds as well—on grounds economic, social, and political. Political independence does not depend on language alone, as the independent German States best prove. What applies to the West can be applied to the East. Of course, Western history shows that the individuality of dialect became subordinate to the cultural advantages derived from the union with the larger and more cultured nations; in France, for instance, Provençal differs from literary French more than the Ukrainian differs from the Russian. Even the German Plattdeutsch and other dialects show a greater difference from the literary language than there exists between the Ukrainian and Russian. It is true, of course, that the French and German literature and culture are richer than the Russian, and France and Germany have not proceeded against their dialectic individualities so foolishly as the Russian Tsarism.

Politically, the Ukraine herself, in the Third "Universal," acknowledged the Central Russian State, and declared herself to be a part of the Russian federation; it is natural that the politically unripe body of the Ukraine felt the need of leaning on Russia. Only later (the Fourth "Universal") the Ukrainian Rada declared the Ukraine to be an independent State not connected with Russia; in that, of course, it had the backing of the Germans and the Austrians. The Pangermans in Germany and Austria did not forget the Ukraine, encouraging the Ukrainians to play an anti-Russian part.[5]

Austria employed the Ruthenians of Galicia (and Bukovina) not only against Russia but also against the Poles, and she looked upon the Ukraine as a fertile soil for her clerical imperialism. (Szeptycki's memorandum.)

41. Not only the Ukraine but Poland and the other small nations in the East need the support of a strong Russia; otherwise they easily, while apparently independent, could come under the deciding economic and even political control of Germany. It will be a matter of great importance how far these nations in the East will manage to agree among themselves (the relations between the Ukrainians and the Poles, between the Poles and the Lithuanians, and between the Lithuanians and the Letts).

The relation of Germany to Russia is the relation of Prussia to tsarism; we have already stated that Prussian theocratism had been at one with Russian theocratism. Austria joined Prussia and Russia (the Holy Alliance,— the influence of Metternich's system in Russia and Prussia —the protection given to the Habsburgs in 1848-49 by Nicholas I—the Alliance of the three Emperors), but the old antagonism of Rome and Byzantium and the Jesuitic policy of Vienna in the Balkans brought about the crisis, and, in the end, the prospect of booty (territory) changed the Russophile policy of Bismarck and Treitschke.

The Pangermans, partly under the influence of Baltic

---

5. For example, "The permanent Russian danger may be abolished in any case only by the formation of an Ukrainian State, and thereby our doubts regarding the Polish question will be solved."—Prof. Jaffe, 1917.

"Whoever wants to overcome Russia must carry the fight to the Ukraine; whoever wants to destroy Russia, or to injure it severely, must take away from her the Ukraine."—Garierre, 1917.

politicians (Schiemann, Rohrbach, and others) drove
official Prussia against Russia; the adherents of the Bismarckian tradition proved to be the weaker. Emperor
William himself, together with Bethman-Hollweg, at the
beginning of the war, accused Russia of being the principal cause of it, and denounced her imperialistic Panslavism—an extremely onesided and incorrect explanation.

Germany's relations to Russia have been changed by
the new orientation of world politics, as they were extended into Asia and Africa. Here Germany came into
conflict not only with Russia but also with England and
France, the principal Asiatic Powers. That brought about
the understanding of Russia with England. The new
German world politics is substantially the consequence of
the old German *Drang nach Osten;* William continued
the Turkish policy of Frederick the Great but under new
conditions. As long as the Germans pushed merely against
the zone of small nations, and as long as the relations of
Prussia to Austria were not definitely settled, Germany
(Prussia) and Russia could be friends, the interest of
both being purely continental, which fact made an agreement possible. Germany had in Russia a near and advantageous market for her energetic industry. As soon as
Germany, after 1866, came to an understanding with
Austria, and as both Berlin and Vienna became more
active in the Balkans and Turkey, and when Germany
embarked on colonial politics, and thereby made Africa
as well as Asia the direct object of her plans, then France
and England were brought nearer to Russia. Russia now
took on a different significance for Germany; the weakening of Russia and the annexation of the Russian South-
west (fertile soil, coal, Black Sea) became the new Ger-

man policy, and the policy of the present war. The annexation of Western Russian Governments, the juggling with the Baltic Provinces, with Poland and the Ukraine, all that is the result of aiming at the organization of a German Central Europe and domination in Asia and Africa. Berlin-Bagdad was broadened to Berlin-Warsaw-Kiev-Odessa. The East, Russia, and the zone of small nations would mean far more to Germany than parts of the West (Belgium, Alsace-Lorraine, or parts of France). Controlling the East, Germany would be enabled to conquer the West. Europe and humanity need an independent and strong Russia.

Russia cannot for some time make herself felt as a military force; Napoleon's prophecy of a Cossack Europe has not been fulfilled; Europe is marching toward liberty and humanity. Russia, striving to be a republic and a democracy, will help Europe a great deal, and does help, although the excessive negativeness of her revolution weakens this influence on Europe more than the shortsighted Bolsheviks imagine. In the meantime Russia needs the help of the Allies.

Russia gained influence in Europe through Pushkin, Tolstoy, Turgenev, Dostoevsky, Gorky; Russia will also have a great political influence if she carries out the revolution consistently, the revolution of heads and hearts. With Russian Tsarism will fall the tsarism of Vienna and Berlin, a more dangerous species of tsarism because it uses science and developed capitalism. The tsarism of the Romanoffs was without culture and brutal, and for that very reason less noxious. The tsarism of the Russian masses and revolutionaries is worse; they rid themselves of the Tsar, but they have not yet ridden themselves of tsarism.

18. WHAT ABOUT A CRITICISM OF THE ALLIES?

42. Someone will raise the objection that I am criticizing the Germans and Austrians and have not a word to say about the Allies.

In doing so I would be formally justified; the Germans, not the Allies, offer themselves as teachers, leaders, the saviors of nations and mankind, and therefore it is our duty to scrutinize them carefully, especially when they force their culture upon us by way of their heavy artillery. The German is a peculiar mixture of a schoolmaster and a bully; he will give you a soul-gladdening sermon and then hit you with his fist in the eye or he may do it the other way round

I would have enough to say concerning the French, English, Americans, and Russians, and could find plenty to criticize; I proved that by my work on Russia and by my critical activity at home. I have never been a national chauvinist; I have not even been a nationalist; I have stated frequently that nationality appealed to me from the social and moral side—the oppression of nations is a sin against humanity.

The sense of my arguments is not, and cannot be, that we should approve without reserve either of the French, or of the English, or of any other Western culture. The question at issue could be only as to a synthesis of all the elements and the component parts of culture worked out by all nations. That in fact is done by philosophers and specialists of all nations, and that is done, too, by many ment, practically, who have the opportunity of becoming acquainted with various nations. Internationalism is not only the easy communication with foreign nations, but its cultural synthesis.

In this synthesis will also be included the German part, and it will not be a minute part; but as far as the political element of this synthesis is concerned, we cannot accept German Prussianism and Austrianism; we have to turn our faces to the example of the French, American, and English democracies: the general principles, not all the particulars, must come from the West.

We are told that one nation, one State, must be the leading, the principal State. Granted; but it must be *primus inter pares,* not above the others; the organization of Europe must be democratic, not aristocratic. The medieval idea of the aristocratic, theocratic imperialism is superseded by the philosophical, ecclesiastical, political, and social revolution of the modern age.

The modern age? We are really in a period of transition, and all of us suffer from the defects, the halfway stage of this transition; the new era will come, and let us hope that this war, which compelled all mankind to revise its history and its efforts, will induce all nations to labor in an enlightened manner for themselves and for all mankind. History, as far as we know it and learn from it, has existed for only a few thousand years; what is that in comparison with the infinite number of centuries of life which the astronomers promise to our planet? Humanity is, indeed, at the beginning of its development; the philosophers of history in all nations declare that the epoch following the Great Revolution, political and philosophical, to be the beginning of an entirely new era; this war and its horrors will shake our consciences and make us accept this conviction.

In spite of the fact that the historical development follows a definite law, the freedom of such decision is not taken away from us; lawful determinism is not passive fatalism. *Velentem ducunt fata, nolentem trahunt*. . . .

43. Even when one is scientifically conscientious, it is
too much to expect that a philosophical attempt toward
the understanding of the war will be free of the personal element, of personal sympathies and antipathies.

Since my youth I have tried to become acquainted with
the accomplishments of all nations. Besides the foundation given me by my own nation, I learned to know not
merely the classical world but also the principal national
cultures of the present day; being brought up also in
German schools, I learned diligently and much from men
of genius like Lessing, Goethe, and others. At the same
time I penetrated into the French and Anglo-Saxon world
—the French and English philosophies (next to the classical, principally Plato's) were my teachers; only later
did I understand the German philosophy, especially
Kant's.

As to the Slav world, I owe much to the Russians and
Poles, also to the Jugoslavs. The Italians also, and the
Scandinavians, enriched my store of knowledge and
widened my horizon.

All my life I was an assiduous, passionate reader and
a conscious observer of contemporaneous world happenings. If I had to say which culture I considered to be the
highest I would answer, the English and American; at
any rate, my stay in England during the war, and a very
critical observation of English life convinced me that the
English, as a whole, come nearest to the ideals of humanity. The same impression was made upon me by
American life. I do not say that the Anglo-Saxon civilization is to me the dearest—that is another question; I see
and appreciate the faults of the Slavs, but I love the

Slav's faults and virtues. I was always attracted by France and her spirit, even though I criticized and condemned much, as I condemn our own national faults and defects.

The German spirit I always respected, but seldom have I felt at home with it. It does not inspire me. Prussia especially I cannot love; but I strive to be fair to her. If I really hate anything, it is Austrianism—or rather Viennism, that decadent aristocratism, chasing after tips, gratuities, that false, mean Habsburgism, that nationally nondescript and yet chauvinistic medley of people known as Vienna. I do not like Prussianism, but still I prefer it, with its robust militarism and hungry harshness of the parvenu, to the thin-blooded, pleasure-seeking spirit of Vienna. Even Tsar William, with his amateurish talking and with his pretended conniving with Providence, unwittingly did more for democracy than the taciturn, "bloodthirsty sovereign," who believed himself, and was regarded by others, to be the most perfect aristocrat of the world—a man mean to the very core.

I have hope that of my German friends a part, at least, will agree with me.

19. THE SIGNIFICANCE OF THE CZECHO-SLOVAK STATE FOR THE LIBERATION OF EUROPE

44. In the Pangerman literature much attention is paid to the Czech question, and the Pangerman politicians are totally hostile to the Czechs and Slovaks, as the views of all of them, from Lagarde to Winterstetten, prove. Mommsen formulated the Pangerman aims when he harangued his countrymen to break the Czech's hard skulls. We Czechs carefully watched, therefore, the de-

velopment of German politics, and especially the Pangerman plan of Central Europe, and when the decisive moment came we took a stand against it.

The geographical location of Bohemia and Slovakia
in the very center of Europe gives to our nation a significant position; Bismarck said that "the master of Bohemia
is the master of Europe"—the Pangerman politicians
often quote this statement of Bismarck. Bohemia, with
Slovakia, interferes with the Berlin-Bagdad plan; the
shortest road from Berlin to Constantinople, to Salonika
and Trieste leads through Prague or through Bohumin
(Oderberg); to Vienna and Budapest, also, the shortest
connection from Berlin is by way of Prague and Bohumin
—Bohemia and Slovakia block the direct connection between Prussia and Austria and the Magyars.

The Czechs constitute the westernmost wedge driven
into the German body; they constitute the farthest West
in the zone of the small nations; they are the western
outpost of the non-German nations in the East. The
Czecho-Slovaks are not a Slav remnant like the Lusatians,
for they have held their own against German aggression
toward the East for more than a thousand years; the
Czechs have opposed the Germans from the seventh century, from the original foundation of their State, up to
the present day. The Slavs of the Elbe and Saal basins
and of the Baltic shores have been Germanized or ex-
terminated; the Czechs maintained their individuality.
To be sure, they are surrounded by the Germans on three
sides; toward the South they border on the Magyars, in
the East on the Poles and the Ukrainians—a very difficult position in a world of national struggles, resembling
the position of the Germans, of which the Pangermans so
loudly complain.

45A. The Czecho-Slovak nation has from its very beginning manifested considerable strength in opposing Germany and Austria; the first Czech State (Samo in the seventh century) reached as far south as the territory of the Slovenes, and a great Moravian Empire also reached as far south as the Serbocroat lands. Later, the Czech State, as we have remarked, actually passed through a period of something like imperialism.

Bohemia did not unite with Austria and Hungary until 1526, in a personal union; from the seventh to the sixteenth century, for a full thousand years, it constituted an independent State. The union with Austria and Hungary was brought about by the Turkish danger; all three States had a common dynasty, otherwise remaining independent; but it is well to emphasize that Hungary in 1526 was overrun by the Turks, only Slovakia remaining free and being included in the union; Hungary had to be reconquered from the Turks by the united efforts of Bohemia, Slovakia, and Austria, which was done after a struggle of nearly two hundred years.

The account of the development of the Bohemian-Austrian-Hungarian union is very interesting and instructive, if we study how the mighty position of the dynasty, judged by medieval standards and reflecting the glory of the Roman Empire, led to absolutist centralization and Germanizing unification; it has already been pointed out that it is not correct to look upon Austria as an illustration of the principle that small nations and States must necessarily federate. The principle of federation was betrayed by Austria.

Legally, Bohemia is still an independent State. The union with Austria and Hungary in 1526 gave it only a common sovereign; the Habsburgs centralized and partially Germanized Bohemia and Hungary only *via facti*, the legal foundation not being affected. The Habsburgs, as Bohemian kings, strengthened absolutism according to the Spanish example in the administrative sphere, but they did not dare to change the legal basis of the compact concluded between the kingdom and the dynasty. (The estates were at that time the representatives of the nation, and remained such until 1848.) The Bohemian State became absolutist, but remained a separate, independent State. The Habsburgs lent themselves as a tool to the Counter-Reformation, the Hussite movement was suppressed with the assistance of all Europe, the revolution of Protestant Bohemia in 1918 was overcome, and the emperor, with his German councillors, endeavored in every way to weaken the Bohemian lands. In particular, they carried through a unique economic revolution; 30,000 families (among them, Comenius) were exiled from the country, and four-fifths of the soil was confiscated and given in reward to military adventurers and noblemen, who gathered from all Europe, like vultures, and divided the Bohemian booty. A large part of the Bohemian property was taken by the Emperor himself. The people were made Catholic with the help of the dragoons and Jesuits; but the national consciousness was not extinguished; the spirit of opposition was not broken —the peasants of Moravia fought against the imperial army as late as 1775.

Maria Theresa and Joseph II were the first rulers who dared to establish governmental departments, but it was Joseph who provoked also a strong national movement and political opposition in Bohemia (and also in Hungary). After the proclamation of the Austrian Empire (1804), giving expression to absolutist unification, the opposition in Bohemia grew, until finally the revolution of 1848 compelled Ferdinand (April 4, 1848) to declare a partial restoration of the Bohemian constitution and independence. Bach's absolutism introduced centralization once more. At the beginning of the constitutional era, made necessary by the defeat of 1859, Emperor Francis Joseph vacillated between centralization and federalization, but leaned more and more toward the former; in 1861 he promised the Czechs, with whom the Germans of Bohemia were at that time at one, that he would be crowned King of Bohemia; in the same year he promised a Slovak delegation freedom and support against the Magyars.

But the promises were never fulfilled. The defeat of 1866 compelled the dynasty to grant concessions, but those concessions that would weaken absolutism the least; the emperor reached an agreement in 1867 with Hungary, or, rather, with the Magyars, by which he granted hegemony to the Germans in Austria and to the Magyars in Hungary. The Czechs opened a radical constitutional opposition by their well-known passive resistance, boycotting the Central Parliament. Emperor Francis Joseph took a personal share in this struggle, and attempted to crush the opposition by force and by the grossest violation of law, but in vain. And so he made an attempt to reach an agreement with the Czechs. He twice issued a rescript to the Bohemian Diet (1870-1871), in which he promised that he would assume the Bohemian Crown, and in which he recognized the historical rights of the Bohemian State, but the Magyars and Prussians, as was recently reconfirmed by the Hungarian Premier, Eszterhazy, prevented the consummation of the agreement. Again the Czech nation fought

against Vienna, until in 1879 the fight ended in a compromise, which guaranteed the Czechs certain cultural
and national concessions (for instance, the University),
but the struggle for the rights of the Bohemian State
was not settled. The Czechs did not recognize the centralistic constitution of Austria, and took part in the
work of the central parliament only under the reserva-
tion of their State rights.

Such is the state of things even today. Austria, having
been transformed into the dual State of Austria-
Hungary, represents the organized violence of the German minority in Austria and the Magyar minority in
Hungary. From the legal point of view, dualism is disloyalty, and actually a conspiracy of the dynasty with
the Germans and Magyars against the Czechs; Austria
came into existence by the union of not merely Austria
and Hungary but of the two States with the Bohemian
State. As a matter of fact, the Czechs are just as fully
entitled to independence as the Magyars; or, rather,
more so, for when Bohemia united with Austria in 1526
Hungary, as noted above, was overrun by the Turks,
only Slovakia being free.[6]

Bohemia was even then, and is today, the "pearl of
Austria"; the military and financial burden has rested
on the Bohemian lands; Czechs, Slovaks, and Austrians
had to liberate, with their blood and treasure, the rest
of Hungary, which only in the second half of the nine-

---

6. In a letter to Helfi, editor of the Magyar paper, *Magyar Ujsag,*
dated November 8, 1871, Louis Kossuth made the following statement:

Between the legal titles which form the foundation of the right of
the dynasty to the throne in Hungary and Bohemia there is not
merely an analogy but a complete identity. That is true of their origin
and time, method, conditions and principles, as well as their literal
wording. The Bohemian land is not a patrimonium, no so-called
hereditary land, no mere appendage of Austria, but a land which
may appeal to diplomatic negotiations and mutual agreements. It
is a State, just like Hungary.

teenth century became stronger and more influential economically. The economic strength of Austria depended wholly upon Bohemia.

The centralistic constitution in Austria and the dual system have never received the sanction of the Czech nation; about these two points turns the fight of Bohemia against the Habsburgs and Austria; on the basis of their right which has recently been recognized three times by Emperor Francis Joseph, the Czechs are an independent nation and State. Austro-Magyar violence does not create a state of law, and limitations do not run against the rights of a nation so long as the nation continues to fight for those rights.

45B. In this war the Czecho-Slovaks, as an independent nation, acted independently—they did not follow the perjured emperor, but took their stand on the side of the Allies.

The Czech nation elected the Habsburgs to its throne; it has the full right to withdraw its allegiance to them when they have proved faithless to the nation. They proved faithless when Francis Joseph acted against his solemn promises to the detriment of Bohemia's rights; therefore the nation since 1848 has been fighting the crown and those provinces and nations (Germans, Magyars) which combined with the crown against it. The Czech nation did not approve the role which the Habsburgs played more and more openly since 1866 as the retainers and servants of Berlin; the Czechs expressed in a solemn manner their attitude toward the threatening Prussianism in 1870 when they, alone of all the nations, officially protested in the Prague Diet the separation of Alsace-Lorraine from France.

In the Vienna Parliament the Czechs defended not

merely their own rights but also the rights of other nations, Slavs and Latins; during the Balkan war they openly supported the Jugoslavs against Vienna and Budapest. They continued in this national and democratic policy when Francis Joseph declared war on Serbia and, as a result of it, on Russia; the entire nation condemned this war. The Czech soldiers manifested this opposition by refusing obedience, by deserting and by joining the Allied armies. This movement, and it is necessary to emphasize this fact, was spontaneous and truly popular; the Czech soldier-voters refused obedience to the Habsburgs. In all Allied and neutral countries numerous Czech and Slovak colonies with equal spontaneity proclaimed the rights of the Czech nation to independence and organized military legions; all these colonies, far exceeding in number a million people, became an organized body under the leadership of the National Council with headquarters in Paris. This National Council, being well in contact with the nation and its leading statesmen and having the approval of the whole nation, in the declaration of 14 November 1915 proclaimed the Habsburgs deposed from their royal office and announced their determination to fight against them. Francis Joseph answered by a bloody reign of terror.

In Bohemia the whole nation by its actions approved the policy of the National Council abroad and solemnly declared on several occasions through its representatives that it demanded full independence and the severance of all ties with Austria-Hungary.

In the meantime prisoners of war increased the original legions into considerable armies in France, Italy, and Russia; on all battlefields Czechs and Slovaks distinguished themselves by bravery and military discipline which was enhanced by the democratic constitution of this their first army. The march from the Ukraine across Siberia became an epic of this war.

The Allies recognized fully the importance of the Czecho-Slovak armies, and of the whole nation, for their cause; the French, Italian, British, American, Japanese, and other governments recognized the army as part of the Allied Armies and the Czecho-Slovak National Council abroad as the Provisional Government of the independent Czecho-Slovak nation.[7]

A consequence of this recognition and its practical confirmation is the relief expedition of the United States and the Allies to Siberia. By these acts the Allies have given the Czecho-Slovak question the importance of an international question; the ravings of German and Magyar journalists and official declarations of the Austro-Hungarian and German Governments against this recognition merely emphasized the international importance of the Czecho-Slovak question.

The press in Austria-Hungary and Germany at first suppressed all news of the Czecho-Slovak movement; only occasionally, for the purpose of intimidating the population, official reports of executions and confiscations of property were published, but in the end the Czecho-Slovak Army and its deeds could no longer be ignored. The Viennese Government, upon the occasion of the Allies' recognition of the National Council and the Army, issued a statement (August 17, 1918) that

7. It should be noted that, since this manuscript has been completed, a bloodless revolution has taken place in Prague on October 29, and the National Assembly, summoned to Prague on November 14, elected unanimously the President of the Czecho-Slovak Republic, confirmed Dr. Beneš in Paris as Minister of Foreign Affairs, and General Štefanik as Minister of War, and formed a definite Cabinet with Dr. Kramář as Premier at the head.

the National Council was a committee of private individuals without a mandate from the nation; the statement says further that the Czecho-Slovak Army cannot be recognized as one of the Allied Armies in the sense of international law, because there is no Czecho-Slovak nation (to wit, an internationally recognized nation); besides, the Vienna government claims that it is a matter of common knowledge that a very small part of the army consists of Czechs and Slovaks. Therefore, in spite of the recognition by the Allies the Austrian Government would treat the Czecho-Slovak soldiers as traitors.

This declaration of the Viennese government is purely Austrian—mendacious and false. The National Council is not a committee of private individuals, and the Vienna protest itself proves that, for such an official declaration would not be issued against a committee of private individuals. In reality the National Council is the organ of the entire Czecho-Slovak people, and it worked and proceeded in accordance with the plans and desires of the national leaders at home, who in numerous declarations adopted and approved the policy of the National Council abroad. The National Council is the political organ of the entire Czecho-Slovak nation. That the Czech lands are legally independent in an international sense is proved by history and by the oaths of fealty of the Austrian rulers as crowned kings of Bohemia; Francis Joseph on four occasions recognized in a solemn manner the historical rights of the Bohemian State.

It is a lie that the Czecho-Slovak Army is composed of very few Czechs and Slovaks. We understand that Vienna would like to have the world believe that Russians and other allied contingents are in this army, but in reality the whole army consists of Czechs and Slovaks, and this army (in France, Italy, and Russia) numbers considerably more than 100,000 men. This means that all Czecho-Slovak soldiers who enjoyed the freedom of decision have proved themselves opponents of Austria-Hungary; and if that part which is under German and Magyar pressure had enjoyed a similar freedom, then the entire nation would have ranged itself openly on the side of the Allies. When the Czecho-Slovak army in the Ukraine fought the invading Austrians the Emperor sent his plenipotentiary to negotiate with them and to induce them to return, promising full amnesty.

The threat that captured men will be treated as traitors does not scare the Czecho-Slovak army; it issued a proclamation that for every life taken a life will be exacted from German and Magyar prisoners, and that for every execution the Habsburgs and Hohenzollerns will be made personally responsible.

After Vienna, Berlin also made an official statement. The Minister of Colonies, Solf (according to a report dated August 22), spoke in a contemptible manner of the Czecho-Slovak Army as a band of robbers without a country; yet after the defeat of the Germans at Bakmach the German general asked this band for an armistice, and in 1866 the Prussian army, when it invaded Bohemia in the war against Austria, officially recognized the rights of the Czech nation to independence and promised to help obtain it. The Czechs at that time considered the Prussians to be more dangerous than Austria; from which time the Czechs and Slovaks became convinced that the Habsburgs were mere servants of Prussia, and therefore renounced allegiance to them. By the same right by which the Habsburgs were elected kings of Bohemia they ceased to be kings—the nation elected them, the nation now dismissed them. Count Czernin in the above-mentioned memorandum properly admitted that the Czech nation was of all the Austrian nations least devoted to the dynasty.

46. This makes it plain that the Czechs will not be satisfied with the concession of national autonomy within an Austrian federation; the Czechs have a historical right to the independence of the Czech lands (Bohemia, Moravia, and Silesia); they insist on the right to the independence of the State created by them. In addition to that, they have a historical and natural right to the addition of Slovakia, so brutally oppressed by the Magyars. (The Magyars have a proverb: *Tot nem ember*— the Slovak is not a man.) Slovakia, formerly the center of the Great Moravian Empire, was torn away by the Magyars in the tenth century, and was later for a short time connected again politically with its kinsman and was for a time independent. Culturally the Slovaks remained constantly in close relation with the Czechs. The Magyars depend culturally on the Slovaks. The union of the Czechs and Slovaks is therefore a legitimate demand. The demand was made not only by the Czechs, but also by the Slovaks. The Slovaks will employ their own dialect in the schools and in the public administration; there can be no language question, because every Slovak, even without an education, understands Czech and every Czech understands Slovak. The Slovaks gave the Czechs in the period of their national renaissance a number of great authors (Kollar, Šafarik), and educated others (Palacký, and, in a measure, also Dobrovsky). The Magyars, though weaker culturally than the Slovaks, attempt to magyarize the latter systematically and bru-

tally; this magyarization was not the natural result of
a cultural preponderance, but was merely artificially
maintained by the administration, which resorted to violence and corruption, exploiting economic advantages. It
is known that the Slovak, and so also the Roumanian,
elections to the Parliament end in pitched battles, in
which non-Magyar electors are simply shot down.
That is the reason why the Hungarian Parliament is
Magyar, though the majority of the population is non-
Magyar.[8]

47. The Pangermans make the most of the cultural
level of the German nation as an argument for its right
to world domination; if culture is a necessary condition
of political independence, then the Czechs and Slovaks
deserve independence fully.

Independent Bohemia early achieved considerable
progress in schools and in education; the Bohemian
State was organized firmly at an early date and its administration in the hands of trained officials was excellent.
Therefore, Bohemia managed to hold its own against
Germany. Agriculture and industry were highly developed. Culturally the Czechs have won renown through

---

8. The Slovak language is an archaic dialect of the Czech; the difference is only in the archaic forms and in a few additional words. The
Slovak language has the same accent as the Czech and the accent is the
distinguishing mark of Slav tongues. Polish, Russian, and Jugoslav languages have each a different accent. Slovak was introduced as a literary
language at the end of the eighteenth century, at the time of the national renaissance of the Czechs and Slovaks; the popular spoken language appealed to the people more than the written Chekh, which
remained the language of the Slovak Lutheran Church. Among the
Czech and Slovak literary men there arose a sharp dispute about the
use of the Slovak, some Slovaks themselves, for instance, Kollar and
Safarik, being opposed to it; to-day, these disputes have practically
ceased, there being no language question for the younger generation on
either side. The unity of the nation and State is in no way menaced
by the use of Slovak.

their Reformation, they being the first nation to resist the medieval theocracy supported by the German-Roman Empire. From Prague University, the first university in Central Europe, there came forth John Hus, who by his martyr's death inspired the whole nation to resist the medieval theocracy of Rome. With Hus the entire Czech national thus opened a new era.

In the Hussite period the Czechs distinguished themselves not only as warriors ("every Czech a captain"); alongside of John Zizka, the founder of modern military strategy, we have Hus, Chelcicky, and Comenius, the teacher and educator of nations. The Czech national church, the Unity of the Brethren, according to the common judgment of history, was an attempt to put into practice the ideals of the purest Christianity. The Czech Taborites (the radical Hussites) made an attempt to practice Christian communism.

Rome and the Habsburgs, this time backed by all Europe, crushed the Bohemian Reformation; Bohemia, weakened by many wars forced upon her, united with Austria and Hungary, but this union, aimed at the Turkish menace, was employed by the Habsburgs for the suppression of the Czech Reformation. The anti-Catholic revolution of 1618 ended at the White Mountain in Jesuit darkness; but traditions of former power and independence and the progressive ideas of the eighteenth century, especially of the French Revolution, inspired the Czech nation to a new spiritual and national life; the end of the eighteenth century marks the beginning of the renaissance of the Czechs and Slovaks as an organic part of the renaissance of all the nations of Europe. In spite of the constant struggle against the perjured dynasty, the Czech nation is today culturally and economically one of the most progressive nations. It has thus proved its virility, its energy and ability to hold its own against the pressure of imperialistic Germany and Austria; this high degree of culture, as we have emphasized before, being attained by the Czechs through their own strength, without assistance from the dynasty and from Austria.

Insofar, therefore, as culture is an argument for political independence (the administration of the State, especially the democratic administration, being facilitated by the enlightenment of the people), the Czechs and Slovaks can employ this argument with full justification, for they are not less cultured than their oppressors, the Germans and Magyars.[9]

48A. The Czecho-Slovak State will have an area four times as large as that of Belgium, and its population would number about 13 millions, of which the German, Magyar, and Polish minorities would number over two millions.

Though we advocate the principle of nationality, we wish to retain our minorities. That seems a paradox, but it is on the very principle of nationality that we wish to retain them. Bohemia is a unique example of a nationally mixed country. Between the Italians and Germans, for instance, the ethnographical frontier is simple and sharply defined. Not so in Bohemia; in a great many places (mines, etc.), and in all the cities, there are considerable Czech or German minorities. The Germans object that the Czech minorities in North Bohemia are "only" working men—people who live on German bread; but this

---

9. Even according to official statistics, there are fewer illiterates among the Czechs than among the Germans.

antisocial argument is obviously false, and it is inconsistent with the process of the industrialization of Bohemia, which, of course, needs factory "hands"; moreover, it was the Germans themselves who invited the Czechs to come, preferring the Czech working man to the German.

The question of national minorities is of capital significance not only in Bohemia but in almost all countries, almost all States being nationally mixed. Even if the new Europe cannot be remodeled on a strictly nationalist basis, the national rights of the minorities must be assured. This will be done in Bohemia. The Bohemians have always claimed equal, not superior, rights. Owing to her central position, it will be to Bohemia's interest to grant full rights to the Germans and the two smaller nationalities. Common sense will demand it.

So far as the German minority is concerned, the eminent Bohemian leader, Dr. J. Grégr, proposed a rectification of the political frontier; parts of Bohemia where there are only a few Czechs might be ceded to German Austria. In that way the German minority could be reduced considerably; but it must be remembered that there are large Czech minorities in Lower Austria and Vienna (half a million); there are also Czechs in Prussian Silesia, in the territories of Glatz and Ratibor, and a large Serb minority in Lusatia. The Pangermans cannot, therefore, justly complain of the fate of the minority in Bohemia. The just rule for the national redistribution in Europe consists in the fair application of the principle of the majority. "Which is the more just—that 10 million Czechs should be under foreign rule, or that $2\frac{1}{2}$ million non-Czechs should be under Czech rule?"

If the Germans insist on the argument that their culture invests them with the right of ruling the less-cultured nations, the fact must be emphasized that the Czechs are not less cultured than the Germans.

There is one means, of a more financial nature, which might help to rearrange national minorities. The German and Austrian politicians, especially the Pangermans, have very often proposed that the various States should undertake a systematic intermigration of national minorities. I see that in England Mr. Buxton recommends this means for the Balkans. It may be doubted whether this expedient would be very effective, if equal national rights were granted. The Magyars tried some years ago to repatriate the small Magyar minority of the Bukovina; the undertaking was a complete failure, for the repatriated colonists soon left Hungary and went back; but after the war many countries will need men—farmers, artisans, and other professional classes, and therefore a systematic transplanting of minorities might be attempted.

The Poles are found in Silesia (about 230,000); with good will on both sides—and that is necessary in the presence of a common enemy—it is possible to find a suitable frontier; the Polish minority could be reduced, especially if the Czech district of Ratibor, in Prussian Silesia, were returned to Bohemia.

The Magyar minority in Slovakia is balanced by the Slovak minority that will remain on Magyar territory.

Some Czech and Jugoslav statesmen point to the possibility of uniting Slovakia with Jugoslav territory; that part of Hungary stretching along the Austrian frontier belonged at one time to Slovakia; today it is German and partly Magyar, but it contains Slovenian and Croatian minorities; this territory, joined in the north to Slovakland and in the south to Jugoslavia, would connect the Northern and Southern Slavs. This zone would be about 200 km long. This plan supposes complete victory of the Allies, and there is no doubt that the Germans and Magyars would not agree to such a plan willingly; but if there is a truly democratic reconstruction of Europe, then the Northern and Southern Slavs will be secure even without this connection.

48B. Recently a new plan has been devised by the Ukrainians living in Hungary; their representatives in the United States wish that their nation would join the Czecho-Slovak State as an autonomous federated part. The proposition must, of course, be ratified by the people in Hungary. These Ugro-Russians, as they call themselves, have been very much oppressed by the Magyars; they number about half a million.[10]

48C. Economically and financially Bohemia is acknowledged to be the "pearl of Austria," and she will in the future be as rich as she is now; she will, in fact, be richer, because she will not have to support the economically weaker provinces of Austria.[11]

Bohemia was, from the beginning of the union with Hungary and Austria, the political backbone of Austria; the Alpine countries were poor, Trieste and the sea were of little importance, Hungary had no economic significance at all. Bohemia exported grain and manufactured goods; it was only in the second half of the nineteenth century that Hungary became the granary of Austria

---

10. There is a party among the Hungarian and Galician Ukrainians who call themselves Carpatho-Russians; they also proposed to the Czecho-Slovak National Council the union with the Czecho-Slovak State.

11. It should be noted that the finances of Austria rest upon Bohemia-Moravia-Silesia, Lower Austria with Vienna, Northern Styria, and, in recent years, on a part of Western Galicia.

and partly of Bohemia, which, until then, like the rest
of Austria, imported the grain and flour she required
from America.

At present the population of the Bohemian countries
is, in round numbers, half agricultural, half industrial.
In Bohemia proper 35 percent are employed in agriculture, the rest in industry, commerce, and the so-called
liberal occupations. In Moravia and Silesia 50 percent
live on agriculture, in Slovakia a much higher percentage
still.

In the years 1906-1914 the average production of
grain was (in round figures), in Bohemia 54½ million
cwt, in Moravia 24 million, in Silesia 4 million.

After making due allowance for grain used for sowing
purposes and for grain wasted, this works out an average
of over 810 lbs. a year per head in Bohemia; in Moravia
the average is 890 lbs. per head. The Bohemian lands
altogether give an average of 815 lbs. per head for a
population of little less than 10 millions, while in the
rest of Austria it is hardly 541 per head. It should be
remarked that half of this grain can be used for milling,
giving flour and foodstuffs of excellent quality, which,
together with the yearly produce in potatoes, peas, lentils,
vegetables, and excellent fruits, is more than sufficient to
feed the whole population. In 1914 the harvest was so
good that it gave an average of 839 lbs. per head. It
should be remembered that the cultivation in Bohemia
has not reached the same stage of development as that
of Denmark or Belgium; there are great possibilities
ahead if the rate of development evinced during the last
ten years is maintained.

During the years 1906-1910 Bohemia and Moravia
contributed almost 46 percent of the total grain pro-

duced in Austria, 41 percent of the potatoes, 44 percent of the clover and fodder, and 93 percent of the beet sugar. The Austrian sugar industry is almost entirely confined to the Bohemian lands. The statistics of the production of fruit, vegetables, cereals, etc., are equally indicative of Bohemia's importance; and this in spite of the fact that these lands represent only 26.4 percent of the soil of Austria and 35½ percent of her inhabitants. Cattle breeding in Bohemia, Moravia, and Silesia has recently been largely improved; the provision of milk and meat is more abundant than in other Austrian countries (except Vienna, which in many respects has the favored position of the capital).

To the total amount of brown coal produced in Austria (26¼ million tons) Bohemia alone contributes 83 percent, and to the 15.8 million tons of black coal 86.66 percent. These results place Bohemia among the richest States in the world, and along with England and the United States and Germany, for she produces about 26½ cwt of black and almost 51 cwt of brown coal for every one of her 10 million inhabitants.

Of the iron ore turned out by Austria (27 million cwt) about a third is produced in Bohemia. Though the country itself is not very rich in iron ore, yet in consequence of the great production of coal, the ironworks in Bohemia are very extensive, forming over 60 percent of the entire industry in Austria. As these two branches of natural wealth and industry are the most important of all, the Bohemian lands are invaluable to Austria.

In the other industries as well, the importance of Bohemia is equally paramount. She monopolizes 93 percent of the entire sugar industry, and about 46 percent

of the breweries. Hops are grown only in the Bohemian
lands, whence they are exported. The engineering industry also has its seat chiefly in Bohemia, as do the textile
(cotton and wool), glass, paper, and leather industries,
stonecutting and grinding, graphite quarrying, chemistry,
and electro-technology.

In consequence of this industrial activity, Bohemia
returns the highest profits for railways, the post, and
telegraphs. Her network of railways is the thickest, and
she alone, out of the whole of Austria, can boast of
private railways run for the benefit of particular factories. This feature is especially characteristic of the
north of Bohemia. The Bohemian postal system yields
52 percent of the total profits.

In banking and exchange the Bohemian lands used to
be dependent upon Vienna, but they have been emanci-
pated since 1895, and during these 20 years the capital
of the Bohemian banks has increased sevenfold, having
risen from 4 millions to 33 million crowns; and it must
be remembered that the chief source of the banking
capital of Vienna is the trade with the Bohemian lands.
The development of the Bohemian trade has, during the
last few years, been exceedingly rapid.

The Slovak territory in the north of Hungary is
different. It is mostly agricultural, as yet comparatively
undeveloped, and as the country is very hilly and the
methods of cultivation obsolete, it is much poorer than
the other Bohemian lands. The southern part, being less
hilly, is fertile enough, producing, indeed, very good
wheat and wine; and as the hilly north has much natural
wealth in the form of iron ore, great forests, etc., which
are, as yet, unexploited, the country could be industrial-

ized to great advantage. It could supply the other Bohemian lands with commodities of which they are short,
such as iron ore, copper, gold, and tin; and, finally, the
country is good for sheep and cattle raising. This territory is very similar to Silesia, the larger part of which
is now industrial, and could be turned to the same use.

Nor must we forget the wealth of the compounds of
uranium and radium, mined at Joachimsthal, nor the
baths of Karlsbad, Fransenbad, and Marienbad, Tep-
litz, Podebrady, Msené, Luhacovice and Pistany. The
Bohemian lands are, in this respect, one of the richest
in the world. In short, except for salt, mercury, and
naphtha, the Bohemian lands have an abundance of
everything necessary for cultural development, so that,
as an independent country, they would be quite self-
sufficient, and would, moreover, be able to export not
only their agricultural but a great part of their industrial
products as well.

From the point of view of modern political economy,
Bohemia may be said to be an ideal country; she has
great possibilities of realizing that harmony between
agriculture and industry, that economic self-sufficiency
which, according to many theorists, enables the forming
of small autonomous States. (Cf. the chapter on Free
Trade in Gide's *Political Economy*.)

In emergencies such as war the Bohemian lands would
also be able to hold their own, both agriculturally as
well as industrially.

The natural and industrial riches of the Bohemian
lands, making possible a very heavy system of taxation,
have always formed the financial foundation of the
Austro-Hungarian monarchy. The population of the
Bohemian lands is much denser, and the whole standard

of life is much higher, than that of the other lands of Austria.[12]

The following table illustrates the Bohemian contribution on the basis of direct taxation to the Austrian finances:

The Bohemian lands pay—	Percent	Other Provinces (except Lower Austria) pay— Percent
House property taxes	49¾	50¾
Tax on earnings	61¼	38¾
Income tax	56·7	43·3
The total of all direct taxes	57	43

The Bohemian lands and the other Austrian lands (not counting Lower Austria and Vienna) have 25.04 million inhabitants, in the proportion of 40.5 and 59.5 percent respectively. Lower Austria is placed separately, because it contains Vienna as the capital, and is thereby privileged; it is also the real center of the Bohemian industry and export trade. Many Czech undertakings have their central offices and rights of domicile there, because the scale of taxation and the municipal rates of Vienna are lower than in Bohemia.

That explains why the ratability of Bohemia tends to drop, while that of Vienna and Lower Austria tends to rise. If we could include those figures in the statistics, and if we entered, in the archives of the Bohemian lands, the precise ratability of those Bohemian undertakings that are domiciled in Vienna, the difference would be still more in our favor; but even as it is, the ratability

---

12. The real Bohemian lands constitute 26·4 percent of Austria, and provide 35½ percent of the whole population. In these lands there are 128 people to the square kilometer, as opposed to 83 in the rest of Austria.

of the Bohemian lands is 11.90 crowns per head, whereas in the rest of the Austrian lands it is only six crowns.

Still more significant are the statistics of indirect taxation in Austria (taxes on beer, sugar, spirits, salt, paraffin, tobacco, and excise taxes, etc.); with the exception of spirits, the consumption of all those articles is far greater in the Bohemian lands.

The Bohemian lands are, indeed, the "pearl of Austria," not only from the point of view of agricultural and industrial production, but also, and as an inevitable result thereof, from the financial standpoint. In the other lands of the Monarchy, the State expenses are greater than the income received from them in return, and this deficiency is made good by the Bohemian countries. In view of the foregoing facts, few people will entertain any doubts as to Bohemia's chances of being self-supporting and progressive.

Bohemia has no seaboard (except in one of Shakespeare's plays), and that, no doubt, is a great drawback as compared, for instance, with little Denmark and the other sea-bordered countries; but Bohemia does not stand alone in that respect; she is no worse off than Serbia, Hungary, and Switzerland. The example of Switzerland shows that not only political idependence can be preserved, but also that modern means of communication enable even a landlocked country to maintain a flourishing industry. Switzerland has not even any coal and iron, and yet she has succeeded in becoming an industrial country. Bohemia, on the other hand, is very rich in coal, and will, therefore, be able to run the necessary railways; but she will have at her disposal Trieste, which, it may be presumed, will be a free port; and she will also have the Serbo-Croatian ports and Polish

Danzig, should her relations with Germany prevent the use of Hamburg. The distance from Prague to Hamburg is the same as that to Trieste; Danzig is a little further, as is also Fiume. There is a possibility of creating a cheap waterway by a Moravia-Oder-Vistula channel, of which there already exists the beginning.

The sea undoubtedly also furnishes comparatively strong strategical frontiers, yet the development of modern navies and airplanes easily counterbalances that advantage, as has been experienced in this war. Belgium, Denmark, and Norway, for instance, can make little use of the sea.

Bohemia would take her share of the Austrian public debt contracted before the war, but she will decline to participate in the debt resulting from the war. The financial situation of Austria-Hungary is very precarious; the war has cost the country an enormous amount of money, and the Austro-Hungarian bank has been degraded into an institute for false coining.[13]

Independent Bohemia would have to begin her own administration with a considerable financial burden; and the leading political men of Bohemia are well aware of their serious task, and of the necessity for a solid, thoroughly balanced financial administration. It may be mentioned that after the war the financial exhaustion of all the nations will necessitate the most stringent financial administration; but it may be said, without exaggeration, that Bohemia will have excellent administrators in all departments of public and private service, who will be quite fit for the work of remodeling the State.

---

13. The bank since the beginning of 1917 has not published its gold account. Bohemia would introduce the franc currency, which combines the Latin and the Russian currency: 20 francs $= 7\frac{1}{2}$ roubles ($40 = 15$).

In this outline it is impossible to discuss all the social and economic problems of Bohemia. But it is of general interest to point out the peculiar position of the Bohemian landed proprietors (aristocracy), which is very similar to that of the famous East Elbian Junkers. As in East Prussia the Germans confiscated the soil of the Slavs, so did Austria and her aristocratic accomplices in Bohemia after the battle of the White Mountain. It was as a result of these and former robberies that, in Bohemia, landed estates were created of a size equal to some of the small German States. These proprietors, for the most part, are Austrian in sentiment, and would perhaps form a dangerous element. Bohemia might, in that case, follow the methods of land purchase and parceling adopted in Ireland, as, indeed, all the Liberal parties demanded before the war.

The Czecho-Slovak State will undoubtedly be a republic.

This very war revealed sufficiently the reactionary and dangerous character of continental monarchism; the Czecho-Slovak nation is ripe for a republic. In the course of centuries we became accustomed to living without kings of our own; the Habsburgs were to us always foreigners; the aristocracy also became estranged from the nation and attached itself closely to the foreign dynasty. The aristocracy in Bosnia-Herzegovina became Turkish and in Bohemia Habsburg.[14]

The independence of the Czecho-Slovak State is a demand of political justice, by its geographical location

---

14. Count Czernin, in one of his memoranda submitted to Francis Ferdinand, charges the Czechs with having the least sentiment for the dynasty. We gladly record this denunciation of this nobleman of Bohemia and Bohemian descent, who years ago publicly declared himself to be a German.

in the center of Europe and by its century-long struggle against the German "Push toward the East," the Czech and Slovak nation is the anti-German vanguard of all the nations in Eastern Europe. Should the Czech-Slovak nation remain in the sway of the Germans and Asiatic peoples allied with Germans, Magyars, and Turks, and should it actually fall, Pangerman Central Europe and its further political consequences will be realized. The Czecho-Slovak question is a world question and is the problem of this very war; free Bohemia or reactionary Austria, the free Czecho-Slovak nation or the degenerate Habsburgs—that is the choice for Europe and America, for the thinking Europe and America.

Her geographical position in the center of Europe, and her historical antagonism to oppressive Germanism and Pangermanism, secure to Bohemia that great political significance recognized since by the Allies; and it is in the interest of the Allies to liberate Bohemia if Prussian militarism and German lust to domination are to be crushed and the Pangerman plan of Berlin-Cairo and Berlin-Bagdad are to be frustrated. The Allies' plan, like that of the enemy, is a far-reaching program. The war and its consequences are the greatest event in human history. The Napoleonic wars, the Thirty Years' War, the Crusades—all these were child's play compared with this war. Realist politicians and statesmen must grasp the inner meaning of German and European history; they must comprehend the direction in which history is pointing, and what Europe's aims and objects can and must be.

I do not maintain that the liberation of Bohemia is the most vital question of the war; but I can say without exaggeration that the aims proclaimed by the Allies can-

not be attained without the liberation of Bohemia. Her
future will be the touchstone of the Allies' strength,
seriousness, and statesmanship.

20. THE CZECHO-SLOVAK STATE, UNITED POLAND, AND JUGOSLAVIA

49. The restoration of the Czecho-Slovak State is only
a part of the task which Europe, or rather the Allies,
will have to undertake in reorganizing eastern Europe;
together with the Czecho-Slovak State there must arise
an independent united Poland and an independent united
Jugoslavia. Of all the acute national questions in the
zone of small nations these are most acute and they are
questions that are closely connected internally.

Between the Polish and Czecho-Slovak nations there is
a strong national and cultural kinship. Under the same
or similar conditions given by their geographical situation, the Poles and Czechs developed for a long time
along parallel lines. Being neighbors they have been in
contact from the very beginning; even in the oldest days
their relations were friendly; sometimes they were un-
friendly, but the relations were always there. The two
nations even had kings in common. Cultural and literary
(even language) reciprocity was strong at the beginning
of the modern era.

The Poles occupy the same position with reference to
Prussia that the Czechs occupy with reference to Austria. Prussia (Frederick the Great) is the real author
of the plan to divide Poland. The unification and restoration of Poland will be the most impressive defeat of
Prussian militarism which has been directing the Pangerman pressure toward the east. Bismarck rightly said

that Posnania was more important to Germany than
Alsace-Lorraine. We see with what energy Prussia op-
poses a "Greater Poland," as the German publicists
expressed it. From Berlin to Bagdad the road crosses
Bohemia and Slovakia, but it may also lead across
Poland; Berlin-Prague-Belgrade-Constantinople-Bagdad,
and also Berlin-Warsaw-Odessa-Bagdad.

Austria made concessions to the Poles in Galicia and
by its anti-Russian policies it gained the sympathy of the
Poles in Russia and elsewhere; in spite of that Austria
is an enemy of the Poles and a more dangerous enemy
than the Poles have heretofore admitted. Austria maintained a very demoralizing system in Galicia; it used
the Ruthenians against the Poles, the Poles against the
Ruthenians, but it did not oppose the policy of extermination urged by Pangermanism (Von Hartmann: exterminate!) and practiced in Prussia. Russia, it is true, also
acted brutally toward the Poles, but it was not so dangerous as cultural Prussia. Mickiewicz, in his famous
Improvisation, stated very correctly the qualities of the
three executioners of Poland.

The Pangerman alliance of Prussia-Austria makes the
interests of the Czecho-Slovaks and Poles identical. Without a free Poland there will be no free Bohemia—without a free Bohemia there will be no free Poland. This
reciprocity and parallelism of political development may
be traced throughout the entire history of the two
States; I will call attention only to the connection of
Grünwald with the contemporaneous national uprising of
Bohemia; at that time, in the fifteenth century, the Hussite movement and the strengthening of Poland held up
for a long time the march of the Germans to the east.
The consequences of the White Mountain were felt even

in Poland—between the respective events of 1620 and
1771 there is a clear connection; the weakening of Bohemia by Austria reached its climax under Maria Theresa and made the partition of Poland easier.

In the Austrian Parliament the Czechs and Poles frequently worked together; the accord was not complete,
but this war must open the eyes of the leaders of both
nations; the common danger of the present and the future
must unite both nations in a common and well-defined
policy.[15]

50. The connection between the important Jugoslav
question and the Czecho-Slovak and Polish questions is
formed in the common danger caused by the Pangerman
plan of Central Europe, which makes for the preservation of not only Austria-Hungary but also of Turkey.
The Jugoslavs are in the South what the Czecho-Slovaks
and Poles are in the North—the vanguard against German and Magyar aggression.[16] The Slovaks no longer have
any common frontiers with the Jugoslavs, but centuries
ago they were immediate neighbors, until the incursion
of the Magyars into the former Panonia separated the
two nations; now Slovak islands extend all the way to
the Serbian border, while Croatian colonies previously
mentioned reach across German and Magyar territory
along the Austro-Hungarian frontier as far north as

---

15. There is an old Polish saying about the friendship of the Poles
with the Hungarians; these Hungarians were really Slovaks, as was
pointed out to me by a Polish historian, who noted that, in reports of
relations of Polish and Hungarian armies, there was no mention of
interpreters, which would have been necessary if the Hungarian armies
had been only Magyar. (I have already mentioned that Hungary, in
the sixteenth and seventeenth centuries, so far as it was not under
Turkish rule, was identical with Slovakia.)

16. Recently the term "Jugoslav" has found general acceptance to
designate the Serbians, Croatians, and Slovenes; therefore I use the
term, even though it is not exact, for the Bulgarians are also Jugoslavs.

Moravia, and besides, there are Czech colonies in Croatia. In spite of the fact that Czechs and Slovaks are no longer neighbors of the Jugoslavs, their political, literary, and cultural reciprocity, and more recently also their economic reciprocity, is very close. The common parliament gave opportunity for political cooperation.

The Jugoslavs have fully grasped the fact that an independent Czecho-Slovak State is for them also a vital question; for the Germans and Magyars press against them from the North to secure the domination of the Balkans and the Adriatic. This situation explains why Italy joined the Allies and why the Italians and Jugoslavs are driven toward a political understanding in spite of the disputes about Trieste and the Italian minority in Istria and Dalmatia. The Jugoslavs deserve the sympathies of democratic Europe. The Serbians in Serbia and Montenegro showed in their fight against the Turks for the defense of liberty a wonderful perseverance and ability; their cultural efforts are energetic and their endeavor to obliterate the traces of centuries-long Turkish pressure is sincere and effective. The Serbian nation, and that is true of the Croatians and Slovenes as well, is gifted and very able. The Slovenes excel in industry and idealism, little fearing German preponderance. Up to now the Jugoslavs more than any other nation suffered from being separated into many parts; they were partitioned among five States (Serbia, Montenegro, Austria, Hungary, Turkey, and a small fraction in Italy), and in these States into a dozen administrative provinces. Ecclesiastically, too, the nation is not united; there are Orthodox parts (Serbia), Catholic (Croatians and Slovenes, but there are Catholic Serbians in Ragusa), and Mohammedan (national consciousness—Servia—is awakening only in recent days), but consciousness of nationality and a desire for unification do not suffer thereby.

The anti-Slav and anti-Serbian politicians of Vienna and Budapest used these differences (*Divide et impera*); Aehrenthal's scandalous diplomacy, that would not stop short of falsifying documents, revealed to the whole world the moral level of Austria. The unification and liberation of the entire Jugoslav nation is surely one of the principal demands of a future free Europe; Austria provoked this war by her anti-Serbian and anti-Russian hatred, and that itself is a sufficient argument for reducing Austria to her German Alpine provinces.[17]

21. A SLAV BARRIER AGAINST PANGERMANISM

51. Liberated and united Poland, liberated and united Bohemia with Slovakia, liberated and united Jugoslavia, so the Pangermans complain, will be a barrier against the Germans; the Poles directly against Prussia, the Czechs and Slovaks against the Prussians, Austrians, and Magyars, the Jugoslavs against the Austrians and Magyars. In a certain sense this is correct—a common and inveterate enemy, pushing with all his might against these nations, naturally and necessarily unites them, but this barrier has a clearly defensive character. These three Slav States will not be buffer States; this concept will have no meaning in a democratic nonmilitaristic Europe, where all nations will be good loyal neighbors.

17. As I picture it, Montenegro will cease, after the war, to be an independent State. Various historical individualities (Serbia-Croatia-Slav Istria-Dalmatia-Bosnia-Herzegovina, Montenegro) might at first remain administrative units and develop gradually into a more closely united State. Montenegro might at an early date be attached to Serbia, Slav Istria and Dalmatia to Croatia.

This barrier is given by history and by the position of these nations in the zone of small nations; these three Slav nations, hardened by the age-long fight with the Germans and Magyars, are destined in the coming new democratic era to be the natural barrier against German aggression toward the East—and the Germans will be compelled to limit themselves to German territory.

But the Roumanians and Italians also have realized the threatening danger and have therefore joined the Slavs, even though there have been national quarrels among them; one, therefore, must not speak of a Slav barrier, the barrier being Slav and Latin, the two races forming a natural defensive league of nations against German aggression.

The Latins and Slavs will further be joined by the Lithuanians, Letts, and Esthonians. The chain of free nations, opposed to Pangermanism, extending from the Baltic to France, is given by history and geography: Esthonians, Letts, Lithuanians, Poles, Czechs with Slovaks, Roumanians, Serbians with Croatians and Slovenes, Italians, and Italians and French in Switzerland.[18] Perhaps even the Magyars will learn wisdom from this war and will realize that the Slavs and Latins will not be hostile to them if they will only limit themselves to their own people. By this natural organization of the zone of small nations the western nations, Italy, France and England, will also have a smaller burden to carry; there will be no fear of German aggression to the West as soon as Eastern Europe is organized politically along natural lines and as soon as Austria-Hungary, the Balkans, and Turkey have been taken away from Germany.

---

18. The population of all these nations numbers over 60 millions.

22. PANGERMANISM AND PANSLAVISM;
GERMANISM AND LATINISM

52. Many Germans, perhaps even Slavs, interpret the war as the conflict between the Slavs and Germans; Kaiser Wilhelm and Bethmann-Hollweg started the agitation for war by instigating hatred against Russia and Panslavism.

That is a onesided and incorrect interpretation of the war. Pangermanism attacked the Slavs in Serbia and Russia, but that is only a part of its program, a step to further aggression against England and France, not only in Europe but especially in Asia and Africa. That England, in spite of its inadequate preparation, decided so promptly to enter the war and to enter it on the side of the Allies is no accident. The war is, as was pointed out, a world war in the full meaning of the term; it is not merely a fight between Germans and Slavs. For that matter many Germans themselves declare today that not Russia but England is their principal rival and foe.

Pangermanism and Panslavism differ substantially. That the various Slav nations feel with one another is natural, for they are close to each other in language and ideas; it is equally natural that small nations expected assistance against the Germans, Magyars, and Turks from Russia; but there has never been an elaborate, aggressively organized Panslavism, or rather Panrussianism, of the type of Pangermanism. We would not reproach the Germans if they sympathized with the Teutons and preached and worked for Pangermanism in the sense of unifying the Teuton race; but the Germans interpret and practice Pangermanism in a directly contrary sense, namely, of having non-German and non-Teuton nations serve the Germans.

Panslavism, preached by Slav philosophers, historians, and statesmen, was, as a rule, satisfied with literary and cultural reciprocity; and if we Czechs have been particularly charged with Panslavism in the sense of Panrussianism, then I must state here the fact that while we have always been decided Russophiles, our greatest political leaders, Palacký and Havlíček, took a most determined stand against Panslavism under the tsarist absolutism. Tsarism itself rejected Panslavism for reasons of legitimacy (Tsar Nicholas I) and for ecclesiastical reasons (it was opposed to Catholics and Liberal Westerners). There is no comparison between political Pangermanism and Panslavism; the latter limited itself, in all its principal exponents, to Slav nations.

France also is Russophile, and England, too, turned to Russia and the Slavs, although it had long been opposed to Russia and paid little attention to the other Slavs; and why are the Japanese aiding Russia, their enemy of yesterday? Why is the majority of the neutrals on the side of the Allies, among them even Teuton peoples (Danes, Norwegians, Flemings, and lately even the Dutch)? Is that Panslavism?

The Pangermans raised nationalism to an almost mystical chauvinism and they impressed upon their nation, intoxicated by frequent military victories, the idea of an elect *Herrenvolk;* against this German danger, heightened by a clever and almost scientific exploitation of the centralized strength of Germany and Austria-Hungary, not only the Slavs but all the other nations made common cause. Their aim, therefore, is not and cannot be only national; it is democratic, being national only insofar as nationality is democratic and social.

For the same reason it is not proper to speak of the struggle of Germanism with Latinism in the West; all nations, and even parts of the same nation, have been until now in opposition and hostility toward each other.

In general it is not sufficient to explain the history and the development of the single nations by the antagonism between neighbors; all nations develop not merely through opposition to their neighbors but also by their own internal forces, and this positive development must also be understood, as it gives to the various nations their individual character. History as the world's court does not pass judgment merely on mutual fights, but also on the internal quality of nations; history that does not go beyond wars between nations, hardly gets beyond quantity, material force, and its contemporary success.

IV. WAR TO THE END

23. THE NECESSITY OF WAR TO THE END IN THE INTEREST OF PERMANENT PEACE

The Problem of War

53. The democratic organization of Europe on the basis of the self-determination of nations presupposes an integral victory of the Allies; unless defeated, Prussian Germany and Prussianized Austria-Hungary will not become democratic, will not permit the democratic organization of Eastern Europe and will stem the longed-for development of all Europe. Austrian and Hungarian ministers declared plainly that they were opposed to the national principle; that is proved, too, by their maneuvres —they are interested in the maintenance of the dynasty and their robber state. Germany, to be sure, supports nationalities when she finds it of advantage to do so, but at home she rejects the self-determination of Alsace-Lorraine, of the Poles, Danes, and others. The true character of Prussianism and Austrianism thus stands out very plainly.

In the interest of permanent peace it is therefore necessary to carry on the war till the end. That does not mean to accept Prussian militarism; we merely demand defense, an energetic and thorough defense.

Defense is psychologically and morally quite different

from attack; the muscular activity is the same in both, but the motives, the entire mental attitude, are quite different. Every act is judged in ethics by its motives, and therefore the defensive war is morally admissible and necessary. Offensive, aggressive war is inadmissible, immoral. Tolstoy's judgment of war is incorrect, in fact his doctrine of nonresistance is incorrect, unnatural, inhuman, under the aspect of humanity, because it prepares victims for men of violence. Truly human ethics demand resistance, everywhere, always, against all evil. Humanitarianism cannot condemn the defensive war; it condemns only the war of aggression.

This attitude, I believe, sufficiently refutes the charge of militarists that democracy in condemning aggressive war leads to passivism and weakening of energy.

The militarists object that it is impossible to decide correctly when war is aggressive and when it is defensive; they claim that the historians have not settled that question even as to wars that were fought out long ago, to say nothing of the present war. Every war may be immoral, so the Prussian militarists will admit after the manner of Jesuits, and therefore one should not introduce questions of morality into it. All this is absolutely false. Historians of Prussia, and of lands where there is no political freedom, cannot solve the controversy; that much is true; and it is also true that certain historians have not the ability for it. But free men of judgment, accustomed to scientific exactness, are able to settle the difference with due exactness. That is true of this war also. Every man sees the difference between defense and attack; all peoples in the world make the distinction between killing in self-defense and murder.

Many pacifists place a wrong valuation on the war.

War is an evil, a great evil, but if we judge by the final effect and the loss of lives and health, it is not the greatest evil: alcoholism, for instance, is probably responsible for as many victims as wars; then there are the effects of syphilis, factory accidents, and so on, which are equally harmful to individuals and to society; the immense number of suicides (in Europe about 100,000 annually) shows clearly that war is not the worst or the only evil; servile life is worse.

Then, of course, there are different ways of conducting war—a bashi-bazouk also makes war; but war in accordance with the Geneva convention is different. The Germans and Austrians have not adhered to this convention and have introduced inhumane methods of warfare; one cannot call them barbarian, because they are planned, the result of that theory of frightfulness which a German officer formulated when he said that he would kill ten thousand children in the enemy country if it would save a single soldier.

Militarism is the real evil which people have in mind, when they talk of the evils of war. Militarism is the mathematics of aggressiveness, the fighting spirit turned into a bureaucratic system—all state activities guided by military considerations, the officer becoming the standard of the citizen and of the world in general. Prussian militarism is universally recognized as the pattern and source of this social evil; the Prussian militarists themselves point out correctly that all life in Germany is militarized. Modern German theologians have made a corporal of Jesus and a drill-master of God.

This militarism is not necessary, as the war itself demonstrates. Not only France but even England stand successfully against Prussian militarism, although England

was not at all militaristic; the armies of the Allies fight
no less bravely than the Germans; and if we consider that
Germany alone was prepared for the war, that German
soldiers are military specialists, the achievements of the
Allied armies are relatively higher than the German successes. Most assuredly this war has already sounded the
deathknell for Prussian militarism; for militarism does
not decide the value of men and nations.

A militia will be a sufficient system of defense for democracy, as is admitted even by anti-militarist socialists
(Engels).

24. WHO IS RESPONSIBLE FOR THE WAR?

54A. From the democratic viewpoint the question who
caused the war, who attacked and who only defended
himself—the question, who is guilty—is of extreme importance. Democracy rests on morality, and for that very
reason the question of guilt is so important.

We do not agree with those who dissociate politics,
and consequently war, from morals, who exalt political
acts, especially of the masses, as something great, something above the small, private happenings in ordinary
life, which are subject to the usual moral standards. My
experience teaches me that men who do not obey the
rules of morality in politics do not follow them in private
life and vice versa.

For that reason also we cannot adopt the attitude of
those Marxists who even in this war appeal to historical
(economic) materialism; "Comrades" Renner and others
insist that war must be judged from the economic and not
from the moral standpoint. Let us grant that; but then
the economic standpoint is not valid for the Germans
only, but also for the Czechs and other oppressed na-

tions. Herr Renner, of course, thinks only of the Germans and their superior rights, and therefore through his materialism he has become a full-blooded Pangermanist; he thinks that "war selection," the force creating the firmest organization, will become the judge, the administrator, and the law-giver of nations. Moltke completely absorbed Marx, naturally; materialism, whether we call it historical or any other kind, necessarily reaches the conclusion that might is right. Herr Renner even now claims to adhere to the *Internacionale,* but it is the *Internacionale* of the German Marxists, as Liebknecht's minority clearly proves, having contracted its scope to meet the exigencies of German militarism and Pangermanism. Herr Renner defends *Mitteleuropa,* and for that very reason he wants to reform Austria-Hungary: he wants to throw a bone to the dissatisfied nations so that they would so much the more effectively serve Berlin as its Eastern vanguard.

Russian Socialists speak often à la Dostoevsky of the guilt of all who fight. I might admit that all are guilty; but that does not dispose of the moral duty to investigate who is the more guilty and who the less. It surely deserves some thought, why all the states before the war looked with connivance on Prussianism and its great strength; without that *tacitus consensus* the Pangerman march to the East would have been impossible.

Quite numerous is a class of historians (principally Marxists) who pretend to be deep thinkers when they claim that in explaining the war one should not look at the causes lying on the surface, but to remote causes, the underlying, real, driving force. It is true that no thinking man is satisfied with secondary causes, with the last causes in point of time, yet not the decisive ones; everyone knows that scratching the match that fired the prepared powder was not the true cause and the decisive motive of the act; but on the other hand we will not be misled by that seeming wisdom, which by means of psychological hocus pocus, such as "the diriving force of driving forces," reveals in fine only economic or similar interests.

A somewhat more modest philosophy of history is preached by those who point to the difficulty of giving a scientific explanation of the war; because of the excessive complication of this question it is not possible to determine the true cause of the war, and historians will not be able to decide that for a hundred years. Certainly the exact statement of all single facts is impossible—certain causes remain unknown, secret archives will reveal in the future many interesting details—but enough is known; on the contrary, such an event as the present world war can be sufficiently explained by the entire development and state of Europe. Today it is already determined with considerable accuracy that Austria and Germany are guilty of the war.

Among the various explanations of this war we find presumably that ultra-scientific positivism minimizing and reducing the moral responsibility of individuals for the war; it accepts historical fatalism as determined by laws in the spirit of passive fatalism and it conceals under the guise of philosophy and history moral indifference and irresolution. Against this unnatural passivism and moral dilletantism, which in real life cringes before success, we join those to whom history is the judge of the world, of individuals and of nations, and who under the weight of world happenings do not lose their faith in moral responsibility and in the duty to help with increased energy in the fight for freedom of nations and humanity.

54B. The analysis of facts makes clear the guilt of

Austria and Germany beyond all doubt; to-day it is already possible to refer to an extensive literature on this question;[1] it is of some importance that in Germany voices are increasing that admit the guilt of Germany and Austria. The author of *J'Accuse* has now among the socialists a number of followers: Bernstein declared that he looks upon his vote for the first military credit, now that he realized the true state of things, as the most unfortunate act of his whole life. The report of Lichnowsky, the journal of Mühlon and other documents, leave no doubt of the guilt of Austria and Prussia; the socialist minority is now strengthened by nonsocialist voices in Austria and Germany, that do not accept any longer, or at least doubt strongly, the official explanation of Berlin and Vienna that the war is defensive. The language of facts is but too clear; Serbia in answer to Austria's ultimatum conceded all that might be demanded of a sovereign state, and Russia placed no obstacles to it; England proposed a conference, and there is no reason why the proposal should not have been accepted—the crowned drones of the Central Powers have usually plenty of time for all kinds of solemn stupidities. Why did not William, Francis Joseph, and Nicholas meet with their chancellors for an oral conference before making such a far-reaching decision?

The spread of Pangermanism in accordance with which the war is not merely carried on, but which was being prepared for years and years, is sufficient proof that Germany and Austria wanted the war, for the Allied Powers were not prepared. The Russian Bolsheviks are siding strongly with the Germans, and yet Zinovjev in his pamphlet considers the German and Austrian preparedness

---

1. In *The New Europe,* 30 November 1916, I wrote a lengthy article on the then existing state of affairs.

as the strongest argument raised against Germany; the more decent Germans themselves admit the strength of this argument—Mr. Harden as early as November 1914 made the candid and emphatic declaration: "We wished this war."[2]

In western literature all guilt, or at least the principal share of it, has been placed on the back of Germany, Austria remaining somehow in the background. This is not correct, Austria's policy in recent years, both before and after the annexation of Bosnia-Herzegovina, was highly aggressive against Serbia and Russia and thereby it brought on the war; Germany in its own interests supported this policy and abused it. The question which of the two is the more guilty need not be discussed here. I merely emphasize that Austria's guilt is great, far greater than its adversaries admit.

Perhaps the objection will be made that Austria acted under the pressure of Berlin; in England, France, and America many people see it that way, and Austria supports and strengthens this legend through its agents. This

2. A member of the Reichstag, the historian Gothein, as early as November 17, 1914, in the *Berliner Tagblatt,* tried to answer the question whether the Germans wished the war, and he was forced to the following admission: "It cannot be denied that certain irresponsible circles played with the thought." Are General von Bernhardi (now one of the most prominent commanders on the Eastern front) and similar writers mere "irresponsible" personages? Herr Friedrich Naumann (*Die Hilfe,* August 1917) explains why the German people no longer believe the war to be defensive.

People can no longer rightly believe that the present battles are inevitable battles of defense. They have rather the gloomy suspicion that a policy of conquest, over and above what is necessary, is being pursued. And here a positively disastrous effect is produced by certain publications in which powerful societies and private individuals give expression to the lust of conquest. Only general ideas of their contents reach the great mass of the people; but to the best of our belief their existence is well known in every barrack, in every workshop, and in every village inn. The consequence of this literature of conquest is the disappearance of simple faith in the defensive war.

is known in Berlin, but it is not objected to; quite the contrary. It is true that Austria is under the influence and pressure of Berlin, but that does not mean that she does not exert any influence on Berlin. In monarchical states mutual personal influences (of sovereigns and their councillors) have considerable weight and in the given case Berlin after 1866 (just as previously) for tactical reasons treated with tenderness the person of Emperor Francis Joseph and complied with his inclinations as much as possible, Austria sometimes having different views. There is a certain tension between the courts of Berlin and Vienna, but both dynasties and their offensive imperialism pointed to the same East, and the bad conscience of militaristic aggressiveness unites the rivals.[3]

The participation of Austria-Hungary, not merely in

---

3. The guilt of Austrian politics shortly before the declaration of war was well brought out by the Berlin *Vorwärts,* when it wrote, July 25, 1914:

We condemn the agitation of the Great-Serbian Nationalists, but the frivolous provocation of the war by the Austro-Hungarian Government calls for our liveliest protest. For the demands of this Government are more brutal than any that have ever been addressed, in the whole course of history, to an independent State, and they can only be intended to provoke war forthwith. The conscious proletariat of Germany, in the name of humanity and culture, raises its burning protest against this criminal agitation . . . . Not a single drop of blood of a German soldier is to be sacrificed to the desire for power and to the imperialistic greed of the Austrian despots.

The rest of the German Socialist newspapers wrote in a manner similar to that of *Vorwärts;* they are cited in an American publication of the German adherents of Liebknecht, "Die Krise der deutschen Sozialdemokratie." Dr. Victor Adler, the leader of the Social Democrats of Austria, admitted in careful but clear words that Austria caused the war when she refused to follow Serbia's concessions with further diplomatic negotiations.

Before him Kjellén, the strongly Germanophile Swedish Austrian, confesses ("Die politischen Probleme des Weltkrieges, 1916") that Austria-Hungary could have solved the Serbian question in a peaceful way, and that the war was not necessary.

Oven, the Orthodox David of the Scheidemann majority, accused the Berlin Government of giving *carte blanche* to Vienna.

the provocation of the war but also in the manner in which it was conducted, is considerable in any case; it is claimed, for instance, quite categorically that not Tirpitz but Burián made the decision for the unrestricted submarine warfare, hoping thereby to save tottering Austria. This is entirely in harmony with the policy of terror through which Vienna hoped to save the internal situation[4]

The responsibility of Germany and Austria for the war is so much the greater because Germany in the very year 1914, before the war broke out, reached a very favorable agreement with England, France, and the other Powers as to controversial questions in Asia and Africa.[5]

---

4. It is worth mentioning that in the various diplomatic blue books of Vienna and Berlin not a word is published about the negotiations of the two Allies from the Sarajevo murders to the Serbian ultimatum. But we see from official statements that both emperors looked from a purely personal standpoint upon the act committed on Austrian territory by an Austrian subject: Austria talked of a punitive expedition to Serbia, and William at the beginning of the war in his frequent speeches plays the role of an avenging Justice.

5. Rohrbach (*Das Grössere Deutschland*, August 15, 1915) says:

Now that everything has changed, we can openly say that the Treaties with England concerning the frontiers of our overseas sphere in Asia and Africa had already been concluded and signed, and that nothing remained but to make them public. We were frankly astonished at the concessions made to us in Africa by England's policy.

In Turkey, he adds, Germany was given concessions in the matter of the Bagdad railway, of Mesopotamian petroleum wells and Tigris navigation beyond all expectations ("ueber-raschend"); and altogether, England was quite willing to recognize Germany as her equal both in Africa and in Asia.

V. THE NEW EUROPE

25. DEMOCRATIC PEACE AND ITS TERMS

Summary
55. Not merely the inborn instinct of self-defense, not merely national sympathies and antipathies, but historical and political insight constrain the Czecho-Slovaks to accept the program of the Allies and to reject the program of the Central Powers.

On the side of the Allies there are found the principal democratic and civilized states, especially the two oldest republics; their opponents—Prussia-Germany, Austria, and Turkey—represent the obsolete, medieval monarchic states, the oldest reactionary forms of theocratic absolutism. On the side of the Allies is the whole world; the Central Powers are morally isolated. The aims of these monarchies are aggressive, militaristic; the aims of the Allies are defensive, pacifist. The German program is anti-national; the program of the Allies is based upon the recognition of the rights of all nations, small and great. The program of the Allies is democratic; the program of the Germans is aristocratic.

The German aims were put into an elaborate system by Pangermanism, and they were followed by the Central Powers in this war politically and strategically.

Pangermanism aims at a German, German-led Central

Europe, the substance of which is formed by Prussian Germany with Austria-Hungary; this latter Empire played in the Pangerman scheme only the role of a German colony, a bridge to Asia. Austria-Hungary is the vanguard of Pangermanism in the Balkans and on toward Turkey. Through Turkey Berlin aims at Asia and Africa.

In the West the Pangermans endeavor to control some neighboring lands, such as Holland, Belgium, the Scandinavian countries, and parts of France and Italy; but the principal concern of Pangermanism is to keep the control of Austria-Hungary and, through it, of Turkey and of the Balkans.

Pangermanism, for centuries pushing toward the East, is now first of all anti-Slav (anti-Czech, anti-Polish, anti-Serbian) and anti-Russian; the weakening of the Slavs and Russia is the first stage of the Pangermanist program; the Slavs and Russia block the road of the Germans to Asia. That is the reason why the Czecho-Slovaks provoke the hatred of the Pangermans. The further plans of Berlin are directed against England and America: the dominion in Asia and Africa is to secure for Berlin the dominion over the West and the entire world.

To overcome the peril of Pangermanism the Allies need determination, energy, and cooperation, not merely during the war but also after the war. The principal task is to compel the German nation to rely on its own strength and to make it impossible for the Germans to exploit the neighboring non-German nations, especially the smaller nations occupying the zone between the Germans and the Russians. That means to liberate and unify the smaller Slav nations, the Czecho-Slovaks, Poles, Jugoslavs, and Ukrainians. The Latin nations, the Roumanians and Italians, must also be liberated and united, and the Allies must at the same time give their full attention and help to the regeneration of Russia.

This national self-reliance of the Germans will be established only if Austria-Hungary is divided into its component national parts. Austria is the principal assistant and accomplice of Prussia and Prussian Germany.

Hence the tactics of Berlin and Vienna in their peace moves to demand the status quo, that is to say, the preservation of Austria-Hungary and Turkey. In fact, it would not be the status quo ante: Austria was saved by Germany from Russia and Serbia and is now only nominally independent; the Habsburgs leaning on their German and Magyar subjects became the obedient servants of the Hohenzollerns. The German nation, the second largest in Europe after the Russians, will not be injured by the defensive plan of the Allies—the principle of nationality, proclaimed by the Allies, will apply to it also; but Austria-Hungary, this anti-national and purely dynastic state, must be dismembered, just as the anti-national Turkey has been dismembered.

Pangerman Central Europe with its political consequence, is an attempt to organize Europe, Asia, and Africa; but this organization is to be carried out by militaristic force, by the domination of the elect German nation over the other nations. The organization of Europe and mankind according to the plan of the Allies is a broader program, a pan-human program, carried out democratically through the self-determination of nations and without militarism. Pangermanism is geographically and culturally a smaller and reactionary program: it aims at the unification of the Old World, Europe, Asia, and Africa. But alongside the Old World there has developed the New World—America. The program of the Allies proclaims the organization of the Old and New Worlds, the direct organization of all mankind.

Every thoughtful democratic and progressive statesman, every enlightened and culturally active nation must accept the program of the Allies, because it is politically broader and culturally and morally higher. The Allies champion humanity, the Pangermans force; the Allies champion progress, Austria-Hungary and Germany are the champions of the Middle Ages. Pangermanism and its Central Europe is a program of the theocratic anachronistic monarchies—the Allies and their program of the organization of mankind is a democratic program constructed logically on humanitarian ideals.

The Pangerman alliance concluded not merely because of geographical and historical reasons, but because of deep inner relationship; Prussia, Austria, and Turkey are in their substance dynastic, militaristic, aggressive, antinational, and anti-democratic. Turkey has fallen. Austria is following Turkey, and Prussia will fall immediately after and through Austria.

The program of the Allies is in its consequences also a program for the liberation and humanization of the German nation.

I. Democracy is the political organization of society resting on the ethical foundation of humanitism; aristocracy (oligarchy-monarchism), as it developed historically, is based on theocracy, on religion and church. European States have not yet freed themselves, all and to the fullest extent, from medieval theocratism.

II. Democracy is a society resting on labor. In a de-

mocracy there are no men or classes exploiting the labor
of others; a demoncratic state does not admit of militarism or secret diplomacy; its internal and external policy
is subject to the judgment and direction of Parliament.
Democracy, it has been said, is discussion; men are governed by arguments, not by an arbitrary will and violence;
democracy today is not possible without science; democracy is the organization of progress in all branches of
human activity.

Democratic states aim at administration, not at domination; they are states without dynasties; the so-called
constitutional monarchy is a transitional form, a mixture
of aristocracy and democracy.

Democracy is the antithesis of aristocracy and oligarchy; monarchy is a form of oligarchy.

III. The discrepancy between State and ethnographic
frontiers causes the unrest and wars in Europe. Nations
are the natural organs of mankind; nationality is the
best guarantee of internationality which, together with
nationality, is the goal of European development. One
conditions the other. States are instruments, the development of nations is the goal. Democracy, therefore, accepts the modern principle of nationality and rejects the
(Prussian) worship of the State and, therefore, of dynasties. The problem is not only to liberate nations, but
also to unify them. The cry of "no annexations" is not
clear; the right of nations to self-determination proclaimed by the Russian revolution demands changes of
political boundaries. The States are nationalized.

IV. Democracy, equally with nationality and socialism,
rests on the humanitarian principle: no man shall use an-

other man as an instrument for his own ends, no nation shall use another nation as an instrument for its own aims. That is the moral purport of the political principle of equality, of equal rights. The so-called small man and likewise the small nations are individualities with equal rights. The socialization of the administration must be supplemented by the socialization of international (interstate) relations.

V. The Prussian State and its kingship, Austria and its dynasty, Turkey and its theocracy are the survivals of the Middle Ages; not only geography, but internal qualities as well, unite these states; Bismarckism, Metternichism, and Djingiskhanism united against democracy and progress.

VI. German, Austrian, and Turkish militarism proceed logically out of dynastical theocratism; the reactionary Pangermanism with its Central Europe necessitates a war to the end. Germany and Austria are guilty of the war; the Allies have the moral duty to defend themselves and the nations that are endangered, and the age-long German "Drang nach Osten" threatens all nations in the zone of small nations between the Germans and Russians. The Hohenzollerns, Habsburgs, and Ohmans, the representatives of medieval democracy and its imperialism, will not accept humanity and democracy unless the absurdity of their worship of the dynastic state and militarism is demonstrated to them *ad ocules*—by a firm manifestation of the will of the allied nations for democracy in the overthrow of theocratic dynasticism, and that means, practically, the smashing of the Prussian militarism at the battlefield. That is indeed driving out the evil by Beelzebub, but no other way is possible so long as force and violence are used and systematized. Defense against violence is a moral duty.

56. 1) The Congress of Peace could convene at once, the war being morally and strategically finished—the nations become convinced that force shall not decide the fate of nations and humanity; even militaristic Prussia must confess that nonmilitaristic nations are equal to it in bravery, in the spirit of sacrifice and even in military ability.

2) The Congress of Peace should be composed of representatives of all belligerent nations, not merely of the governments. Admission should be granted to the representatives of all nations whose fate is being decided and who have a claim to self-determination.

3) The antiquated and insincere diplomatic rule that states should not interfere in the internal affairs of other states should not apply in the coming peace congress; if democracy is truly humanitarian and if the strengthening of international feeling is not to be a mere phrase, then political boundaries must not be a shield of arbitrariness. This terrible war arose just because states have for such a long time avoided interference in the internal affairs of their neighbors.

4) All secret agreements must be excluded.

5) Theocratism must be abolished in all the states of Europe; the churches must be free and they must not be abused for political purposes. The American way of arranging the relations of the state and the church can serve as a suitable model.

6) All states must abolish standing armies and employ for their defense in case of necessity a system of militia (abolishment of militarism).

7) Navigation of the seas outside of territorial waters must be made free to all nations. Exceptions are made by international agreement. To landlocked nations access to the sea must be secured by an international agreement; an ex-territorial harbor and duty-free passage of goods will be granted at the nearest shore.

8) Commerce is free; protection of industry and commerce against unfair competition must be regulated by international agreement.

The doctrine of the old liberalism demanding absolute freedom of trade is often exacted in a very abstract way and is deduced from conditions prevailing in western, civilized industrial Europe (principally England and France). Freedom of trade may be abused by the stronger to the subjugation of the weaker, just as war can; the subjugation may even be worse and more demoralizing. In that manner Austria-Hungary threatened Roumania and Serbia by a tariff war. Every country in the agricultural stage endeavors to become an industrial country and to be economically independent; industrialization implies the growth of a railroad system and of means of communication in general, and that again presupposes a certain degree of scientific education of the nation, practical and theoretical. Every country will want to protect itself against exploitation. From this wider cultural standpoint we must consider the watchword of free trade and international commerce must be wisely and justly regulated for all nations by international agreement.

9) The most difficult task of the Congress will be the just settlement of territorial questions. Owing to German aggressiveness and the Pangerman push toward the East the national questions are most acute in the East of Europe: Prussia, Austria-Hungary, the Balkans, and

Russia must be politically reorganized. The reconstruction of the East is the primary aim of the war and of the Peace. In the West there are no acute disturbing national questions: the nations of the West have their states and well-established forms of government, have their old civilization—France and Belgium will have to rebuild their destroyed cities and villages, to repair their factories and fields, but in the East new states, new forms of governments must be created and the foundation of civilized life must be laid down.

The territorial readjustment of Eastern Europe will, as a rule, be carried out according to the principle of nationality; but in each case due regard must also be paid to present economic conditions, and to historical peculiarities. The great complexity of the national problems makes each concrete national question a distinct political problem of its own.

10) Belgium must be completely restored; Germany must make compensation for the losses caused by its perfidious attack and occupation.

11) The non-German nations of Prussia, Germany, must be liberated.

In the first place, Alsace-Lorraine; though the majority of the population is German, they desire to be united with France, or at least to break away from Germany. Alsace-Lorraine was annexed to Germany in 1871 against the will of the people, and has never become reconciled to the annexation; on that occasion the representatives of the Czech nation alone protested officially against this deed of violence. True, the German Socialists of those days had enough courage to protest also.

The Danes in Schleswig must be united with Denmark, the Poles in Prussian Silesia and in Posnania with

Danzig must be united with their countrymen of Russia and Austria. Eastern Prussia will thus become a German enclave having direct connection with Prussia by the sea.

The Lusatians, should they so wish, may be joined to Bohemia, the Lithuanians of East Prussia (with a few Letts) would be attached to Lithuania. Czechs in Prussian Silesia will be exchanged for German territory of the Austrian Silesia. Prussia and Germany would in that way become unified nationally, something that the Pangermans themselves desire; that is no injury to the German nation, for it would merely compel the Germans to limit themselves to their own national resources and give up exploiting non-German nations.

I have not the least doubt that the Pangermans will reject with the greatest indignation such a solution of the Prussian question—to free the Lusatians? To have within cannon shot of Berlin a free Slav territory? Yes— that would be a victory of justice and Nemesis: if the Allies win, a solution of the Prussian question in a democratic and truly national sense is possible and necessary.

The Germans will object to leaving Danzig to the Poles; they already proposed to give the Poles a free access to Danzig. The Polish population reached the sea banks of Danzig and the sea shore; the forcible, inhuman Germanization of the Slavs justifies such German losses.[1]

---

1. The German professor Schaefer in his ethnographical map (1916) gives the following statistics of non-German nations in Germany— Prussia: Poles, 3,746,000; French, 216,000; Danes, 147,000; Lithuanians, 106,000. These figures are estimated to be too low; Schaefer's map conceals the fact that there are Lusatians and Czechs in Prussia. Some ethnographers, even Slavs, declare the Kashubs are a nation distinct from the Poles, and the Lusatians also are divided into two branches. A more detailed ethnographic exposition is here unnecessary. (There are in Prussia, just as in the Austrian Bukovina, Russian and other colonies, but these questions are without political significance.)

12) The entire Polish nation, in Russia, Austria, and Prussia, must be united into an independent state. It will have access to the seas through its own territory (Danzig).

13) The Bohemian Lands (Bohemia, Moravia, Silesia) with the Slovaks of Northern Hungary must form an independent state. The boundaries of the Bohemian Lands are given, for the Bohemian state is by law independent; the so-called German territory in Bohemia (Moravia and Silesia) has many Czech inhabitants, therefore it is just that the renewed state keeps it; it would be unjust and inhuman to sacrifice hundred thousands of Bohemians to the *furore teutonicus;* as late as 1861 the Germans in Bohemia were one with the Czechs in demanding the coronation of Francis Joseph as King of Bohemia. No doubt, after this war the Germans in Bohemia will abandon the national fury into which they have been driven by the brutal Pangerman agitation. Many Germans themselves more than once protested against the Pangerman policy of severing North and West of Bohemia and trying to establish a new capital in one of the German towns.

Respecting the Magyar minority, it must be emphasized that there are no Magyars in Slovakia, only Magyar-speaking individuals; the Magyars closed the Slovak schools, suppressed the Slovak literature, and are trying by all means to denationalize the Slovaks. It is only just to stop this brutal, inhuman policy and to force the Magyars to rely on their own national forces.

It was reported that the Hungarian Ukrainians (the Ukro-Rusins and the Carpatho-Russians) wish to be incorporated as an autonomous unit in the Czecho-Slovak state. And it was also proposed to connect Slovakia with

Jugoslavia by a kind of a corridor starting at Presburg and stretching south along the boundaries of Lower Austria and Styria to the River Mura; this area takes in Hungarian territory, but is inhabited by Germans, not Magyars, with Croatian colonies and a Slovene minority.

14) The Ukrainians (in Galicia, Bukovina, Hungary) will become a part of the Russian Ukraine.[2]

15) The Magyar nation forms an independent state.

16) The Roumanians of Austria, Hungary, and Russia will be united with Roumania.

17) Jugoslavs form an independent federation, led politically by Serbia. Montenegro will decide, through its parliament, whether it any longer wishes to be independent or united with Serbia.

18) Bulgaria will be recognized within its boundaries before the war; it may be given part of Turkish territory.

19) Albania will remain free. It has been proposed that she may federate with Serbia or Greece or Italy— but that must be decided by the Albanians themselves. Albania cannot have a German ruler or any prince connected with Austria or Germany.

20) Turkey must no longer be allowed to keep any territory in Europe; the Allies agreed on this point in their Note to President Wilson. Constantinople and the Dardanelles will probably be administered by a commission of the Allies; a definite disposition will be made as experiences of the new states will be acquired.

---

2. The terminology in the case of the Ukrainians is embarrassing. *Ukraine, Ukrainians* has been used of the part of the nation living in the south of Russia; in Austria the name *Ruthenians* or *Rusins* has been used. The whole nation is often called *Little Russians,* in distinction of the *Great* (and White) *Russians.*

Not all Ukrainians claim to be a separate nation distinct from the Russians; in Austria and Hungary there has been a political party professing national unity with the Russians and calling themselves Russians (*vide* the mentioned Carpatho-*Russians*).

The Turkish movement, known as Neo-Turanian, a very close analogy of Prussian Pangermanism and Austrian Imperialism, deserves sharp condemnation; the Neo-Turanians appeal to the memory of Djegis Khan— in every encyclopedia you will find that this barbarian imperialist put to death five million people, a horrible figure, but still smaller than the number of victims of the two Pangerman Williams and Francis Joseph.

21) The Greek question (or rather questions) require a careful consideration; it would not be unjust to restore Constantinople and the Dardanelles to Greece— to some degree it is a question of finances, a question whether Greece could afford the cost of maintenance. There are many Greek cities and scattered territories in Asia Minor; they should be restored to Greece.

22) Italy will receive the Italian territories of Austria; Trieste will probably be a free city and port.

Italy points to the fact that her eastern coast in the Adriatic is, owing to its straight shores, in a great disadvantage as against the many excellent harbors of Istria and Dalmatia; this fact and the fact that there is a small Italian minority in Dalmatia are adduced as reasons for annexing a great part of Dalmatia and the islands. Dalmatia would be dangerous to Italy in the hands of Austria led by Germany: it will not be dangerous in the hands of Serbia and the Jugoslavs, because they have no navy and will not be rich enough to build up a dangerous navy; neither have they any aggressive plans. Trieste and Pola will suffice to secure for Italy the supremacy of the Adriatic; Italy's right to these was conceded by Serbia (Pašić's London Declaration); the main problem that Italy will have to solve is and will be the problem of population and finances. Italy very soon will outdistance

France with regard to population; if Italy develops its industries and increases its wealth, it will exercise a decisive influence on the Adriatic and the Balkans through its economic strength. The eventual closing of the Adriatic in the Straits of Otranto depends mainly upon the size and efficiency of the navy. The disposition of the occupied islands in the Ægean Sea must be made by agreement at the Conference.

23) The German provinces of Austria will become an independent state; they will decide whether or not they will join the German federation.

24) Russia will organize itself in accordance with the principle of the self-determination of nations into a federation of nations. In this federation there could in the west (outside of the Poles) be the Esthonians, Letts, and Lithuanians; the Ukraine will be an autonomous part of Russia—their attempt to be entirely independent could sufficiently convince the Ukrainians that separation from Russia will turn them into slaves of the Germans.

The various small nations of the Caucasus and of other parts of Russia and Russian Asia will enjoy national autonomy in accordance with their degree of education, national consciousness, and number. The Prussian part of the Lithuanians (with a few Letts) will be united to Lithuania. The Roumanian part of Bessarabia will be joined to Roumania. Finland may be independent if it reaches an agreement to that effect with Russia.[3]

---

3. The entire independence of the Baltic nations has been proclaimed after the German occupation and the Russian revolution; but representatives of the Lithuanians, for instance, until lately proposed federation with Russia. A close union of the Lithuanians with the Letts has been proposed to facilitate the independence of both peoples.

The Armenians proclaimed their republic and joined the Allies in fighting the Turks and Germans; similar attempts have been tried by some of the small nations in Russia.

25) In the Far East of Asia political supremacy belongs to the cultural nations of the Mongolian race; Western Asia has in fact been a part of Europe and will be organized by the agreement of Russia, France, England, and Italy. Russian Asia will remain united to Russia, English and French Colonies will continue to be English and French; nations under European rule will be secured, in accordance with their cultural development and their number, national autonomy, and participation in the government.

26) Africa will remain substantially under the rule of England and France; Germany may receive back its western colony; Italy will agree with England and France as to the increase of the colonial domain.

27) America (Northern, Central, and Southern) will not permit Germany to establish autonomous German colonies.

28) With regard to colonies, their administration must have regard for the needs of the native peoples and educate them and extend self-government to them gradually.

29) The German colonies in Polynesia will be given to England and Holland.

30) The Jews among all nations will enjoy the same right as other citizens; their national and Zionistic aims will receive after the example of England all possible support.

31) The Congress will adopt a law with international guarantees securing to national minorities cultural and administrative self-government.

32) Ethnographic rectifications of state boundaries may, with the consent of the nations concerned, be carried out from time to time according to the growth of

national consciousness and experience. The Congress must urge an exact census of the population according to nationality, for the existing official statistics are very partial and insufficient.

33) The Congress should provide leading principles for eugenic supervision, secured from the point of view of hygiene, of the growth of the population in all the states; policy in regard to population will be of great importance after the war in all the countries. Alcoholism, for instance, must be suppressed internationally.

34) To secure the execution of the principles and decisions reached by the Congress of Peace, the Congress will transform itself into an international tribunal, controlling the cultural development of nations and the organization of international reciprocity (League of Nations).

The leading principle of all decisions must be the endeavor to facilitate the international organization of all nations of Europe, and to bring them nearer to the nations of Asia, Africa, and America. If necessary, some closer unions of nations can be formed.

The political innovations proposed in this theme are neither many nor surprising. They are in harmony with the development of nations and their just demand of political freedom and unification. *De facto* only two independent states would be new, the Polish and Czecho-Slovak; Bohemia and Poland are not new states, for they had once been free; their freedom will merely be restored. Bohemia is legally independent, Austria and Hungary oppressed by force. The other states will remain, some enlarged, some diminished, or their independence will be strengthened (Finland—Hungary). Of course, Austria-Hungary will be radically changed, and so will Russia and partly Prussia. It is just the transformation of Eastern Europe which furnishes the strongest proof that the world war will end far differently than Pangermanism expected.

But the New Man, *homo Europeus,* will be the result not merely of external politics, but principally of internal. All nations will be obliged, after the war, to devote all their thought to material and spiritual rebirth. Mutual slaughter is not a great action; the belligerent nations will realize the greatness of this moment; they will create a new historical epoch if they rightly appreciate the horrors of this war, if they overcome the war fever, and orientate themselves as to where and how further development should proceed, and if they decide for permanent peace and for humanity. Democracy must become the faith of all, a world view. In Prussia, the Germans organized a forcible germanization of the Poles, and a philosopher was found (Ed. v. Hartmann) who declared in the name of the Prussian ideal the necessity to exterminate the Poles ("austrottcn"); in Hungary the Magyar oligarchy maintained itself by shooting Slovak, Serbian, and Roumanian voters and by the suppression of their schools, the literature, and press; in Austria the Pangermans publicly plotted their schemes of forcibly germanizing whole nations; Russian tsarism followed the German example; civilized Europe remained quiet and acquiesced in all these political atrocities, until this war revealed the danger under which the nations of Eastern Europe were languishing for years and years.

The political task of the democratic reconstruction of Europe must be attained and actually made possible by a moral reeducation of the nations—either democracy or dynastic militarism; either Bismarckism or rational and honest politics; either force or humanity; either matter or spirit!

Prussian and Austrian politicians, the German and Austrian Emperors louder than others, emphasize the religious foundation of their policy and their states; but this religion is political religion. Prussia and Austria are survivals of the theocratic, medieval imperialism; democracy is the antithesis of theocracy.

Religion will not lose thereby its weight of authority; on the contrary it will gain, if it is freed from the state and the arbitrary will of deified dynasties. What was right in the medieval theocracy—the idea of catholicity, universality, mankind as an organized whole—will not be lost by democracy. Democracy also hopes and works to the end that there may be one sheepfold and one shepherd.

Cæsar or Jesus—that is the watchword of democratic Europe, not Berlin-Bagdad, if Cæsar is conceived as Mommsen constructed him, seeing in him the ideal of Pangerman imperialism.

CHIEF WORKS OF
T. G. MASARYK
Chronologically Arranged

Suicide and the Meaning of Civilization. Translated by W. B. Weist and R. G. Batson. Chicago: University of Chicago, 1970. First published, Vienna: Carl Konegen, 1881.

David Hume's Skepsis und die Wahrscheinlichkeitsrechnung. Vienna: Carl Konegen, 1884.

Versuch einer Concreten Logik. Vienna: Carl Konegen, 1887.

"Skizze einer sociologischen Analyse der sogenannten Gründberger und Königinhöfer Handschrift." *Archiv für slavische Philologie.* Vienna: 1887.

The Czech Question. (Czech title, *Ceska otazka.* Not translated.) Praha: Čas, 1895.

Karel Havliček. Praha: Jan Laichter, 1896.

The Modern Man and Religion. Translated by Ann Bibza and Dr. Václav Beneš. Revised by H. E. Kennedy. London: Allen & Unwin, Ltd., 1938. (First published 1897.)

Die Philosophischen und Sociologischen Grundlagen des Marxismus, Studien zur Socialen Frage. Vienna: Carl Konegen, 1899. (Czech edition 1898.)

"Die wissenschaftliche und philosophische Krise innerhalb des gegenwartigen Marxismus." *Die Zeit.* Praha: 1898.

Palackýs Idee des Böhmischen Volkes. Praha: Verlag, JUC, 1899.

Die Bedeutung des Polnaer Verbrechens für der Rituala-berglauben. Berlin: H. S. Hermann, 1900.

Ideals of Humanity. Translated by W. Preston Warren. London: Allen & Unwin, Ltd., 1938. First published, Praha: Čas, 1902.

"Los von Rom." Address in Boston. Unitarian Historical Society, 1902.

Modern National Philosophy. (Czech title, *Národnostní filosofie doby novější.*) Praha: Jičín, 1905.

Ein Katechetenspiegel. Frankfurt: Neuer Frankfurter Verlag, 1906.

"The Religious Situation in Austro-Bohemia," *Freedom and Fellowship in Religion.* Boston: Charles Wendte, 1907.

Freie Wissenschaftliche und Kirchlich gebundene Weltanschauung und Lebensauffassung. Vienna: Carl Konegen, 1908.

Der Agramer Hochverratsprozess und die Annexion von Bosnien und Herzegovina. Vienna: Carl Konegen, 1909.

Vasič-Forgách-Aehrenthal, Einiges Material zur Characteristik unserer Diplomatie. Prague: Čas, 1911.

The Spirit of Russia, Studies in History, Literature & Philosophy. Translated from the German by Eden and Cedar Paul. 2 vols. London: Allen and Unwin, Ltd., 1919. Originally published in German under the title *Russland und Europa.* Jena: Eugen Diederichs, 1913. vol. 3, 1967.

The Problem of Small Nations in the European Crisis. Inaugural lecture, Kings College, London, October, 1915. Council for Study for International Relations. London, 1916.

The Slavs among the Nations. Lecture delivered February 22, 1916, before the Institute of Slav Studies in Paris. Czech National Alliance in Great Britain. London, 1916.

The New Europe. London: Eyre & Spottiswoode, Ltd., 1918.

Sur le Bolschevisme. Geneva: Sonor, 1921.

"The Slavs After the War," *Slavonic Review.* June, 1922.

Les Problèmes de la Démocratie, Essais Politiques et Sociaux. Paris: Marcel Rivière, 1924.

The Making of a State, Memories and Observations, 1914-1918. English version by H. Wickham Steed. New York: Frederick A. Stokes Co., 1927. London: Allen & Unwin, Ltd., 1927.

Speech of T. G. Masaryk, President of the Czechoslovak Republic on the Tenth Anniversary of the Attainment of the Country's Independence, 28th October, 1928. Prague: Orbis, 1928.

"Mein Verhältnis zu Goethe," *Prager Rundschau.* September, 1931.

"Der Grundgedanke der heutigen Ausführung ist: der Weg Zum Glück, Oder aus dem Leben—Für das Leben." Prague, 1932.